MODEL T
TO TESLA

MODEL T TO
TESLA

AMERICAN AUTOMOTIVE VISIONARIES

LIGHTNING
GUIDES

FROM THE
EDITOR

"Nothing behind me, everything ahead of me,
as is ever so on the road."

—JACK KEROUAC, *ON THE ROAD*

No object embodies the American ideals of individuality and open space, of urbanism and utopianism, of freedom and the future, like the automobile. The utilitarian practicality of the Model T; the Space Race-inspired fin-tailed behemoths of the 1950s; the electric supercars of today: automobiles reflect and define our social and cultural gestalt. Around the globe, the automobile expresses our ego and our image. Street-racing American muscle cars with giant engines. Tiny Japanese minicars that reflect the population density of an island nation. Efficient German luxury sedans. Automobiles take on the personality of their place and time, expressing volumes about their designers and their drivers. Created by visionaries and titans of industry, shaped by wars and depressions, driven by natural resources, technology, safety and speed, the automobile is part and fabric of our daily lives, our aspirations, and our dreams.

CONTENTS

INTRODUCTION

Cars are everywhere. Millions of us get into cars every morning on the way to work and when the time comes for us to take a break, our cars take us there too. We can't even cross the street without waiting for a line of cars to go by, and then we pass even more cars that are parked on the sidewalk. No one can deny that cars are ever-present in our daily lives.

But few of us appreciate just how much the automobile—its capabilities, its sales, and its legend—impacts every aspect of our society. Cars dominated American manufacturing throughout the 20th century, and continue to provide millions of jobs around the world. They have literally shaped our landscape, starting with the highway system and leading right up to our doorstep. Cars paved the way for modern factories, and entire cities can rise and fall based on the success of cars. Their factories helped fight war efforts abroad and provided thousands of jobs at home. They're part of who we are: sleeping in the back seat on family trips, getting a driver's license, packing up and moving out, hitting the road just to break free—we cannot imagine ourselves without understanding cars.

How did cars become the backbone of our lives? It wasn't inevitable. Hardworking inventors, engineers, and visionaries dedicated countless hours in a collaborative effort that has spanned centuries. The only way to understand the scope of our achievement is to revisit their journey. So climb in. Buckle up. Turn the key.

KARL BENZ INVENTED THE FIRST *GASOLINE-FUELED* AUTOMOBILE IN

1886

CHINA LED GLOBAL *Production in 2013 with*

22 MILLION AUTOMOBILES

The term AUTOMOTIVE **COMBINES AUTOS** (GREEK, MEANING "SELF") **AND MOTIVUS** (Latin, meaning "MOTION")

15 MILLION MODEL T'S *HAD BEEN BUILT BY 1927*

190,000 AMERICANS were employed by the **AUTOMOBILE INDUSTRY IN 2012**

Which country buys the most cars?
In 2010 some 240 million vehicles were operating in the United States, about 769 vehicles per 1,000 people. By comparison, the world ratio was 148 per 1,000 people.

How did the automobile come to dominate transportation?
American society had made huge leaps in travel and communication by the end of the 19th century. Railroads, canals, steamships, and the telegraph were all carrying new opportunities and innovations across the country. These technological marvels set the stage for the 20th century, yet the invention that sparked the transportation revolution was a simple two-wheeler, the bicycle. The bicycle's popularity in the 1880s and 1890s spurred widespread interest in developing roads—an infrastructure expansion that paved the way for the car's arrival as the dominant force in transportation.

How did the American auto industry get its start?
Oliver Evans was awarded the first automobile patent in the United States in 1789. Thousands of entrepreneurs took part in developing, assembling, and selling automobiles of various scales. As sales increased, production ramped up, as did broader marketing and distribution. Thomas Jeffrey and Ransom Olds were the first American business leaders to begin mass

production of vehicles. Henry Ford, who's often erroneously thought of as the inventor of the car, focused on producing automobiles that were affordable for the American middle class and on refining production methods for greater efficiency.

Who first developed electric vehicles?

Hungarian Ányos Jedlik successfully made a tiny car powered by an electric motor in 1828. Six years later, American Thomas Davenport, inventor of the direct current electric motor, ran his engine in a small car on a track. In the 1830s, Robert Anderson of Scotland invented the first electric-powered carriage, using non-rechargeable primary cells. In England, a patent was granted as early as 1840 for use of rail tracks powered by electric current, and similar patents were issued in the United States in 1847.

What are the trends of consumption when it comes to cars?

Production and sales of automobiles have slowed considerably in many developed nations. Industry watchers predict that the downturn will continue, especially as younger generations eschew car ownership in highly urbanized nations. On the other hand, in emerging markets—particularly Russia, China, India, and Brazil—sales are increasing, as economic growth has stirred demand. These nations account for one-third of all sales, but indicators suggest that even these top markets were slowing in 2014.

How does driving cars affect the environment?

One major environmental concern about driving cars is the impact on air quality. The combustion of gas releases a number of pollutants into the air, including carbon dioxide, one of the most potent greenhouse gases. Oil consumption is another big issue. In May 2012 the Union of Concerned Scientists launched a program called Half the Oil, aimed at reducing usage through the adoption of electric and alternative fuel vehicles.

Are driverless cars the future of the automobile?

Driverless cars, also known as fully autonomous vehicles, have already been road tested in prototype, with projected commercial availability by 2020. Driverless cars could reduce the world's 1 billion autos significantly, especially if self-driving public vehicles become replacements for private cars, which, of course, require drivers and are parked 90 percent of the time.

How did the Ford Mustang change the American automotive landscape?

When it debuted in 1964, introduced to the world by Lee Iococca at the World's Fair in New York, the Ford Mustang became an instant icon. That year, 22,000 units were sold. Four years later, Steve McQueen defined what is was to be cool for a generation, driving a specially designed Mustang through the hills of San Francisco in *Bullitt*.

What's the best selling car of all time?

Though not pioneered by an American visionary, this distinction goes to the Toyota Carolla, which has sold nearly 40 million units since it was first released in 1966.

How did NASCAR influence the New Journalism?

In 1964, when a young Tom Wolfe wrote about Junior Johnson, the country's preeminent NASCAR driver at the time, the *Esquire* story, "The Last American Hero", marked the first instance of Wolfe's signature style of reporting. This style would become known as the New Journalism, and was favored by writers such as Truman Capote.

IT BEGINS WITH BENZ

PIECE BY PIECE, THE FIRST CARS STARTED DOWN THE ROAD TO REALITY

After a fairly inauspicious start in life, German-born Karl Vaillant, later named Karl Benz, drifted through various professions before becoming an engineer and designer in Vienna, Austria. Throughout childhood, Benz was a cyclist and spent much of his youth imagining ways to power his tiring journeys from home to school. When he returned from Austria to Mannheim, Germany, Benz formed a business partnership with August Ritter at an iron factory. When Benz married Bertha Ringer, in 1872, they bought out Ritter and began developing new engine ideas. Benz's goal was to develop a two-stroke gasoline engine, which he finally produced on December 31, 1878, and received a patent soon thereafter.

Benz made many innovations en route to patenting his engine, including the gearshift, clutch, water radiator, carburetor, spark plug, battery ignition, and speed regulator, all of which received patents.

Benz's company was incorporated in 1882 as Gasmotoren Fabrik Mannheim, a legal and financial decision

DID YOU KNOW

The namesake of one of the world's most recognized luxury brands, Mercedes, experienced extreme poverty. Mercédès Jellinek, Emil Jellinek's daughter, left her first husband for a poor sculptor, and died an untimely death at age 39, never having benefited from the success of the company.

that left him a minority stakeholder. When he found that his new partners were ignoring his ideas, Benz left the organization and formed a new enterprise with Max Rose and Friedrich Wilhelm Essingler, called the Benz & Company Rheinische Gasmotoren-Fabrik.

The company focused primarily on industrial machinery and was immediately successful. Benz began exploring his early passion for bicycle technology and turned his eyes towards designing a motorized horseless carriage. He replaced the wooden carriage wheels with wire frames, and designed a four-stroke engine with coil ignition and a cooling system using evaporation (as opposed to a radiator). Benz used a chain system to motorize the rear axle. The final prototype was developed in 1885 and named the Benz Patent Motorwagen.

As Benz developed his engines, many other inventors were focusing their efforts on developing a horseless carriage. French inventors Claude and Nicéphore Niépce—the latter widely known as a pioneer of photography—had created the Pyréolophore, an internal combustion engine that they used to power a riverboat. The engine type was

[
Cars were hardly the only innovations that changed daily life in the 1890s. The decade before the turn of the century also saw the advent of the magnetic tape recorder, the radio, and the steel-framed skyscraper.
]

revolutionary and is regarded as the first of its kind. In 1807 inventor François Isaac de Rivaz had created his own combustion engine, but installed his on a land vehicle. The power for the Niépce brothers' invention came from a mix of plant powder, resin, and coal dust, all mixed with oil, whereas Rivaz focused on hydrogen and oxygen. While neither development had lasting success, the concept fascinated and inspired many others.

As Benz was getting closer to developing his prototype, French-born Gustave Trouvé launched an electric three-wheel car at the International Exposition of Electricity in Paris in 1881. Although the concept created excitement, Trouvé was unable to produce his vehicle and was soon surpassed by the patenting of Benz's Motorwagen. Production began on the Motorwagen in July 1886, and an estimated 25 were sold before 1893— due in part to Benz's wife, Bertha, who undertook the world's first-known car road trip to demonstrate the vehicle's road-worthiness in 1888. When Benz's vehicle was developed with four wheels, it was so successful that Emile Roger began producing Benz engines under license in France, where the machines outsold the German market.

PATENT PENDING

In 1877, New Yorker George Selden designed the first American car with an internal combustion engine run on gasoline, but he didn't get it functional and patented until 1895. The patent for his two-stroke engine hampered other inventors, including Henry Ford, in developing similar engines. Selden's patent was overturned in 1911.

Many developments followed, including Benz's next patent, the Boxermotor—the first flat-style internal combustion engine. By 1899 Benz was the world's largest automotive company, making 572 engines a year, but it was a Czechoslovakian company, Nesseldorfer Wagenbau, that became the first to manufacture factory-made cars, producing the Präsident Automobil in 1897. A few years earlier, German brand Daimler, spearheaded by Gottlieb Daimler and Wilhelm Maybach, launched its first car by adapting a stagecoach for horse-drawn travel, retrofitting the engine, and selling about 30 vehicles.

Although Daimler died in 1900, the Daimler brand engineered a "Mercedes" engine by Emil Jellinek, another German designer, who later named himself Emil Jellinek-Mercedes. The name came from his daughter, Mercédès, who was born in 1889.

Jellinek conceived of an engine that could race, and his Mercedes engine achieved up to 35 horsepower. With Daimler's death, Maybach left the company, and Karl Benz suggested that Benz and Daimler cooperate on developing engines. The outbreak of World War I

Ethel Flock Mobley, along with Louise Smith, competed in the NASCAR Grand National competition in 1949. Mobley's three brothers, Bob, Fonty, and Tim, were early NASCAR drivers. Named after the gas her dad used in his taxi, Ethel ran over 100 Modified stock-car races in her career.

derailed those plans, but in 1924 the two agreed to work together on standardizing design, production, and marketing, despite maintaining respective brands. They merged fully in 1926, creating Mercedes-Benz.

NOT QUITE SPONTANEOUS COMBUSTION

AN EXPLOSION OF ENGINES

The internal combustion engine—commonly called an ICE (ironically, considering that it is a heat engine)—uses force generated by fuel combustion with an oxidizer in a combustion chamber, generating movement. Typically, air is used as the oxidizer, and the force created by high-pressure gases drives turbine blades or pistons. Étienne Lenoir, a Belgian engineer, developed the first commercial ICE in 1859, but it is German-born Siegfried Marcus who is more commonly credited with inventing the prototype in 1864.

Although various engines were developed before these two inventors' time, the earlier engines were hindered until the commercial drilling and production of petroleum began in the

1850s—providing an ideal fuel for the ICE's rapid expansion. Widespread adoption of the ICE was possible by the end of the 19th century, thanks to a range of engineering advances.

External combustion engines, relying on steam, were already in development, but steam wasn't generating enough power in smaller vehicles, as it was nearly impossible to store the water needed. External combustion founded the railroads, but it couldn't be adapted as a personal transportation solution.

Early forms of ICEs included the use of gunpowder, moss, coal dust, resin, hydrogen sparked by electricity, and oxygen to generate needed energy. It wasn't until 1823, when English engineer Samuel Brown developed a powerful ICE based on hydrogen, that the commercial and industrial applications were first considered.

The gasoline ICE was integral to the mass production of motorized vehicles. The achievements of Karl Benz, Gottlieb Daimler, and Wilhelm Maybach pioneered the technique and the vehicle itself. After Benz's wife, Bertha, demonstrated the first long-distance journey using the patented Benz engine, the horseless coach became the focus of a new era of engineering and transportation.

In other parts of Europe, automobile innovation was also gaining traction. Italian-born Enrico Bernardi, though less recognized than Daimler and Maybach, patented a one-cylinder gasoline motor in 1882, fitting it to his son's tricycle, and later designed a vehicle seating two adults.

Meanwhile, in England, Frederick Lanchester developed disc brakes and an electric starter, which, in an adaptation of Benz's starter, became one of the first four-wheel gasoline vehicles, patented by 1895.

HOW
THE MANY
HAVE FALLEN

FROM HUNDREDS OF INDEPENDENT
CARMAKERS TO THE BIG THREE

I n automotive terms, the Big Three refers to the three major car manufacturers in North America—Ford, General Motors, and Chrysler.

For decades, the Big Three were the biggest carmakers in the world, and while each remains in the top 10, only two of them are now in the top five, with Ford slipping from second to third behind Toyota in 2007. In 2008 Toyota supplanted General Motors as the number-one automaker.

Many other carmakers have come and gone from the spotlight. General Motors acquired Buick, Oldsmobile, and Oakland (later known as Pontiac) as early as 1904, and although General Motors continued to produce cars under those names, the smaller companies were liquidated by the acquisition. Ford followed suit by buying the luxury brand Lincoln in 1922. Cadillac was originally part of Ford but became independent before Cadillac was acquired by General Motors.

As Ford and General Motors increased their market share, French-born Louis Chevrolet founded his brand in 1911 in Detroit—though it was taken over by General Motors in 1918. The United Kingdom's Vauxhall Motors, Australia's Holden, and Germany's Opel all had been bought by General Motors by the early 1930s.

Buick's former president, Walter Chrysler, created a new company, Maxwell Motors—soon renamed Chrysler. It took over Dodge, Plymouth, and DeSoto, but retained their brand names, pushing Ford into third place in the market.

Some 30 American manufacturers had produced 2,500 vehicles in 1899, and an estimated 485 companies entered the market in the next decade. In 1908 there were 253 active carmakers, a number that dropped to only 44 by 1929. A full 80 percent of the cars made in the United States was accounted for by the Big Three. The Great Depression forced the closures of most of the remaining independents, with Nash, Hudson, Studebaker, and Packard collapsing after World War II.

World War II created tremendous challenges for the automobile industry. Stutz Motor, Pierce-Arrow, Peerless Motor, Marmon Motor, and Cunningham all failed to survive bankruptcy. Doble Steam Motors and Franklin Automobile, despite early success, also went under. Auburn Automobile and Duesenberg Motors went bust around the same time.

Even the companies spun off from the Big Three, such as Delphi, couldn't survive alongside their former parents and became insolvent, disappearing (or reappearing in various weakened forms) in the ensuing decades.

Right: Chevrolet's marketing efforts touted the powerful and economical benefits of buying a Chevrolet 6, "The six for the price of four." Chevy first started producing trucks in 1918, and the Chevrolet 6 replaced the 4-cylinder engine.

FORD FOLLOWS FUNCTION

FROM MODEL T TO MODEL AUTOMAKER

Although recognized as an inventor, American-born Henry Ford used existing technologies, such as the assembly line, to transform automobile manufacturing through the Ford Motor Company. His achievements include creating the first mass-produced vehicle affordable to the American middle class. His revolution in automotive assembly and production had a sweeping impact on the US and global economies. Ford became one of the most famous people in the world, as well as one of the wealthiest. His vision of "Fordism" is recognized internationally as a standardized form of mass production coupled with employee benefits.

The Ford Motor Company was Henry Ford's second foray into the automobile industry. He founded the Detroit Automobile Company in 1899, but within two years the company failed. Through restructuring and new financial backers, Ford was able to reorganize the company into the Henry Ford Company. A year later, his financial backers fired him, allowing him to take the rights to his name but just $900 in capital.

Left: Ford Motor Company assembly line in Dearborn, Michigan

Undeterred by these setbacks, Henry Ford joined ranks with Alexander Malcomson, and together they drew up designs for a new car company. Again, failure was close at hand, as the pair could not organize efficiently enough to pay for the parts needed for manufacturing. Two brothers, John and Horace Dodge, who had provided most of the parts for the proposed model, were the largest creditors demanding repayment. Malcomson's uncle, John Gray, stepped in to finance and restructure Ford and Malcolmson's endeavor. He brought in investors and persuaded the Dodge brothers to accept stock in the new company in lieu of the monies owed.

Under Gray's stewardship, the Ford Motor Company was incorporated on June 16, 1903, with 1,000 shares divided among 12 investors, including Ford, Malcomson, and Gray. Although Gray had reluctantly taken the role of president, he was immediately rewarded when, in October 1903, the company was declared profitable. By 1905, the profits were almost $300,000.

FORD TAKES THE WHEEL

The success of the new company didn't alleviate tensions between the founders. In 1906 Ford assumed the presidency following the death of 64-year-old Gray. He took this opportunity to freeze Malcomson out of the company, as they'd become increasingly frustrated with each other's differing visions. Malcomson sold his shares to Ford, deciding that with many pending lawsuits against the company over patents, the company could be in jeopardy. The lawsuits were dismissed in 1911.

The Model T—Ford's signature car—was introduced in 1908, when Henry Ford began implementing a mass-production assembly line technique, rather than relying on two or three workers to assemble one car at a time. The new method required moving to a larger plant, which meant greater efficiency by cutting assembly time from almost 13 hours per vehicle to less than three hours, and increasing output to about 202,000 vehicles per year. By 1920, 1 million cars were rolling off Ford's production line annually.

The Model T transformed the American car market. The first to feature left-side driving, the Model T also included an entirely enclosed engine, and its suspension was vastly improved over its predecessor's. The streamlined components made it cheaper and easier to repair, and the model sold at a relatively low $825 (about $21,000 in 2015 dollars). The price fell year after year, allowing thousands of Americans to acquire their first vehicles. Ford's media campaign was intensive, promoting a newly motorized nation. Ford's network of franchises and independent dealers allowed his distributors to profit, and by targeting farmers in rural communities, the commercial benefits of owning a Model T were realized.

The huge increase in production and profit transformed the company, but not the employees. Turnover was surprisingly high, and the increase in factory-line productivity led to a reduced need for labor. To stem the exodus of workers and rebuild morale and loyalty, Ford doubled his frontline employees' pay

[
Founded just outside of Detroit in the suburb of Dearborn, Michigan, in 1903, the Ford Motor Company is the second-largest family-run company in the world, and in 2015 was the fifth-largest automaker globally.
]

to $5 a day and shortened their long shifts to eight hours a day and a five-day workweek. Ford began recruiting workers with disabilities, and loyalty soared while turnover dropped. The higher pay also meant that employees were more within reach of purchasing the products they made.

UNLEASHING ON UNIONS

Despite Henry Ford's seemingly liberal attitude toward the needs of his employees, he was vehemently opposed to organized labor. He refused to allow labor unions within his plants. He made several appointments in the company to ensure that unions didn't gain a foothold. Some of his anti-union appointees—notably his head of security, a former boxing champion named Harry Bennett—arranged physical attacks on union leaders, captured firsthand by a newspaper photographer. The violence against union leaders, who were trying to organize and protect workers, led to stoppages and a downturn in productivity. A strike in 1941 almost led Ford to break up the company. But Ford's wife, Clara, persuaded him to change his mind by threatening divorce if he didn't cooperate with the union. The United Auto Workers (UAW) gained a place in the Ford structure, and production resumed.

[
Henry Ford was awarded the Nazi party's Grand Cross of the German Eagle in 1938. Ford continued to express anti-Semitic views, using a newspaper under his ownership, the *Dearborn Independent,* to publish articles supporting the Nazi agenda. His articles were published in a collection titled *The International Jew: The World's Foremost Problem.*
]

From the beginning, Ford also had an eye on the international market. Having expanded into Canada in 1911, Ford opened assembly plants in Ireland in 1917; England, Denmark, and France in 1923; South Africa in 1924; and Argentina, Australia, Austria, and Germany in 1925.

The Great Depression, which hit all American and global manufacturing, led to a major drop in Ford's fortunes, with mass layoffs and a reduction in output. Ford set up assistance programs for skilled workers newly unemployed in Detroit, providing loans and even land to many of his former workers.

A backlash against the Ford Motor Company and Ford himself included a worker-organized petition demanding more support for the unemployed. As many as 5,000 people joined the Ford Hunger March in March 1932. The march turned into a violent battle with police, injuring 60 people and leaving at least five dead. More deaths resulted overseas when Ford's attempt to enter the Soviet market led to many of his workers in the Novgorod Soviet plant being imprisoned or killed.

As tensions leading to World War II escalated, Ford publicly declared the

DID YOU KNOW

By 1924, Ford was so successful that the company accounted for half of all US sales and half of all British car sales. The Ford assembly line pushed many competitors into bankruptcy, as they either couldn't or wouldn't adopt the Ford model. Of the 200 carmakers in the United States in 1920, just 17 were still in business by 1940.

On July 30, 1938, German diplomats award Henry Ford, center, Nazi Germany's highest decoration for foreigners, "The Grand Cross of the German Eagle", for his service to the Third Reich. Karl Kapp, German consul in Cleveland, pins the medal while Fritz Heiler, German consul in Detroit, shakes his hand. General Motors Corp. and Ford Motor Co. deny helping the Nazis during World War II and profiting from forced labor at their German subsidiaries.

pending war a waste of effort, and he tried in vain to maintain peaceful trade. Jewish workers at Ford's plant in Cologne, Germany, began to be targeted. The Jewish plant manager was fired and replaced by Robert Schmidt, a key figure in the Nazi regime. As fears grew that the Nazis would nationalize the Ford factories, Henry Ford remained close to the Nazi leaders.

When war came in 1939, the Nazi government assumed control of all Ford factories in Germany, and Ford was allowed to retain 52 percent ownership. He immediately helped support the Nazi's buildup of machinery for its armed forces. His other European business partners refused to support the Allied forces with airplane manufacturing, and Henry Ford diverted many rubber supplies from his European plants to help the Nazi military.

Despite Ford's strong support for the Nazi war machine, he did much to support the US military as well, using his company's resources to strengthen President Roosevelt's "arsenal of democracy." Ford's decision to help both sides of the war may have been due not only to business strategy but to his physical frailty and weakened health. At 76 years old, Ford had largely passed the day-to-day control of the company to his son, Edsel. When Edsel died unexpectedly of stomach cancer, 80-year-old Ford returned to run the company. Due to his poor health, leadership transitioned quickly to his grandson, Henry Ford II. The founder died in 1947, at age 83, on his Dearborn estate.

Since 2006, Allan Mullaly has been president and CEO of Ford. During the 2008 financial crisis, Mullaly's company, built on Ford's principle of self-reliance, was the only American automaker not to receive a bailout from the government. Ford's legacy is evident not only in the cars on the road, but in many of the values he engineered into the American identity.

THE FORD FOUNDATION

CHANGING LIVES FROM MAIN STREET TO SESAME STREET

Henry Ford and his son, Edsel, created the Ford Foundation in 1936, using a gift of $25,000 from Edsel. The mission of the foundation was the advancement of human welfare. After the death of both founders by 1947, the foundation controlled 90 percent of the nonvoting shares in the Ford Motor Company, but by 1974, the foundation had sold its shares and today plays no part in the company's operation. The foundation board appointed California lawyer H. Rowan Gaither as the new chair, and he commissioned reports on the foundation's future. Based on Gaither's recommendations, the foundation expanded its outreach and vision through the 1950s.

Since its creation, the Ford Foundation has promoted global education, human rights, creative arts, the strengthening of democracy, and economic empowerment of developing nations. As of 2014 the foundation reportedly had assets in excess of $11 billion, and as of 2011, was granting about $413 million per year. The grants were aimed at reducing poverty, promoting democracy, and alleviating injustice. The foundation is among the largest and most influential in the world.

In 1951 the foundation became heavily involved in creating public-service broadcasting by financing the National Educational

Television, which launched in 1952. The grants continued over the decades, with key innovations financed by the foundation, including the Children's Television Workshop and the globally successful show *Sesame Street*, in 1969.

Under the foundation's Program for Playwrights, regional theater and workshops flourished with the help of grants for emerging writers. Arts and humanities fellowships promoted the works of major artists, including Josef Albers, James Baldwin, Saul Bellow, E. E. Cummings, Robert Lowell, and Margaret Mead. The future secretary-general of the United Nations, Kofi Annan, received a grant from the foundation to complete his studies at Macalester College in 1961.

Civil rights organizations benefited from Ford Foundation grants estimated at $18 million, including the National Council of La Raza, the Native American Rights Fund, the Puerto Rican Legal Defense and Education Fund, and the Southwest Voter Registration Education Project, which expanded access to civil rights litigators for many minority groups.

MUST GO FASTER

AS SOON AS THERE WERE CARS, THERE WERE RACES

Soon after the first gasoline-fired combustion engine appeared, drivers began to test the limits of speed. Official and unofficial racing began with the first event, in 1887, in Paris. Covering just over one mile from the city's

Above: A Bugatti T13 Brescia takes a tight turn at the Prescott Hill Climb, a raceway in Gloucestershire, UK. Prescott Hill still holds races, and is home to the Bugatti Owners' Club. Brescias were manufactured between 1914 and 1920.

Neuilly Bridge to the Bois de Boulogne park, it was arranged by the magazine *Le Vélocipède*. The first official race was a bust, however, when just one car arrived at the starting line. George Bouton drove the race uncontested in his personally constructed car from his own De Dion-Bouton company.

French enthusiasm for auto racing grew steadily. In 1891, at the first Paris-Brest-Paris road race, Peugeot entered Auguste Doriot and Louis Rigoulot to drive their Type 3 model among standard cyclists pedaling their way through the course. The auto company's goal was to publicize the machine and demonstrate its reliability and safety. As the course stretched for 745 miles, it was a genuine test of endurance never before attempted by a vehicle. Doriot and Rigoulot finished the course, but sadly, six days after the winning cyclist had returned home.

The world's first true motoring contest took place on July 22, 1894, when *Le Petit Journal* sponsored a race from Paris to Rouen. Billed as a "competition for horseless carriages," the race attracted more than 100 motorists who paid 10 francs each to enter the race, though only 69 actually arrived to start the 79-mile route. Many of the drivers were simply enthusiasts in vehicles ill-equipped for long distance, so the organizers permitted only 25 to start the race. Many of the bigger French automakers made sure they were represented, with Peugeot, De Dion, and Panhard eager to demonstrate the safety, speed, and efficiency of their models.

The 1907 Peking-Paris race stretched 9,317 miles through fearsome terrain, mainly unsuited for any vehicle, from Peking (Beijing) to France. Only five cars took part, and an Italian driver, Prince Scipione Borghese, triumphed.

The race was very close. Although taking almost seven hours to reach the finish line, via the Bois du Boulogne, Jules-Albert de Dion arrived first. Less than four minutes later, Albert Lemaître crossed the line in his Peugeot. De Dion had averaged 19 kilometers per hour but was disqualified. Lemaître was declared the winner, as De Dion's vehicle had been steam-powered (it needed stoking), which had been clearly forbidden in the race rules.

The Paris-Bordeaux-Paris race of June 1895, covering 732 miles, was completed in just under 49 hours by Émile Levassor in his Panhard-Levassor, some six hours ahead of Paul Koechlin in a Peugeot. Later that year, over the Thanksgiving holiday, the *Chicago Times-Herald* race took place, the first of its kind in America. Six entrants covered the 54-mile route across the South Side of Chicago, generating huge public interest, with Frank Duryea winning in just under 10½ hours. Speed became the key spectator feature of organized races, with "Speed Week" taking place in Nice, France, in March 1897. International competitions began appearing, and courses became more complex, with uphill and downhill elements.

The popular European road races largely ended in 1903 when eight drivers tragically lost their lives in an accident during the Paris-Madrid international race. The French government halted the race and banned all open-road racing.

GETTING ON TRACK

Recognizing that road races posed extreme danger for spectators as much as for competitors, racing organizers in the early 20th century welcomed the arrival of motor-racing tracks. Several US cities created racing venues—the first in Knoxville, Iowa, and a second in Milwaukee. Both tracks had started life as horse-race venues, but car races began in 1901 at the Knoxville Raceway, and in 1903 at the Milwaukee Mile. More tracks appeared on Brunots Island near Pittsburgh, and close by at the Uniontown Speedway.

Across the pond, the British were showing interest in car racing, opening the 2.75-mile Brooklands track in 1907, the first to feature a concrete track with banked corners. Other parts of the British Empire were also keen on racing, and the first Indian competition was raced from Delhi to Mumbai in 1905, covering 810 miles.

The popularity of racing continued to grow, and by the 1930s cars were being designed specifically for racing, resulting in high-priced road vehicles capable of great speed, as well as race cars that couldn't be driven on normal roads. Luxury brands such as Alfa Romeo, Bugatti, Delage, Delahaye, and Mercedes-Benz all

RALLY CRY

Besides track racing, a number of other types of racing have gained immense popularity: off-road racing, rallying, drag racing, and stock-car racing. The annual Baja 1000 race features desert racing, and the Paris-Dakar race is one of the most popular cross-country rallies.

When the Indianapolis Motor Speedway opened in 1909, initially with balloon races, the 2.5-mile track was surrounded by an arena with capacity for 257,000 seated spectators, making it the largest sports venue ever constructed.

Vintage Aston Martin race cars at the Monterey Historic Automobile Races at Laguna Seca Speedway in Monterey, California.

began developing engines with increased horsepower, lighter alloys, and paint-free finishes—reducing weight and drag. As race cars (as opposed to passenger vehicles) became more common, auto-racer Bill France cofounded the National Association for Stock Car Auto Racing (NASCAR). The first NASCAR Strictly Stock race was held in Charlotte, North Carolina, on June 19, 1949.

After World War II, car racing emerged as a leading international sport, as new technology, safety measures, and advances in speed were achieved. NASCAR started a world championship, and throughout the 1950s and 1960s, more international events came to the fore. Larger engines and sleeker designs transformed the sport, with many manufacturers appearing in the market. The IndyCar racing series separated from NASCAR, and more emphasis was placed on open-wheel racing. The single-seater open-wheel championship Formula One (F1) became the most famous racing forum. Among the renowned races held under the F1 banner is the Monaco Grand Prix. The annual championship is staged as much for car builders as for drivers.

Although the goal of all Formula One, Indy, kart, off-road, "drag," and other forms of auto racing is generally speed, efficiency, and technological advances, there's more to the sport than those elements. Historical-car racing is also hugely popular and generally features enthusiasts and amateurs as opposed to professional drivers with corporate sponsors. Cars of all eras compete. Modern safety rules are the only technological requirement for vehicles taking part. Races such as the Goodwood Festival of Speed and the Monterey Historic Automobile Races encourage motorists with vehicles from all eras. Although some professional teams compete in this area, it is generally wealthy hobbyists who participate.

Racing has become enshrined in American culture. A 2014 poll found that racing—including NASCAR and Indy—was more popular with Americans than either hockey or basketball. Internationally, the Monaco Grand Prix is not just a convenient set for James Bond movies, it's also a temporary home to Formula One's dozen teams, which, combined, are worth more than $4 billion. From the moment the first cars rolled off the assembly lines, drivers and spectators alike have wanted to push the limits of speed.

WORLD WARS

THE AUTO INDUSTRY AND
THE WAR EFFORT

I n 1914, the outbreak of World War I had a deep impact on
fledgling automobile industries across Europe and North
America. Although car production was shut down almost
completely in the United States, the major manufacturers
turned their focus to the war effort. Their contributions to

Above: Workers constructing a Martin PBM aircraft, at the Glenn L. Martin
plant in Baltimore, MD, February 1943.

the war rapidly drove technological advances forward, which benefited motorists enormously once the conflict ended.

In the United Kingdom, the Rolls-Royce company had already claimed the largest share of the luxury market, boasting it manufactured "the best car in the world" after the war. Not surprisingly, the British government had enlisted Rolls-Royce into the war effort as soon as hostilities in Europe began.

Rolls-Royce's leading vehicle was the Silver Ghost, but even this sturdy, finely engineered machine needed adaptation for the battlefield. Armor cladding replaced the coach-built bodywork, and many were installed with a rotating machine-gun turret on the engine top.

Aside from its autos used in ground offenses, Rolls-Royce separated itself from its competitors by developing a robust aero-engine division. Although they only offered three engines at the start of the war, and despite their inability to keep up with demand, Rolls-Royce's units powered more than half of the aircraft used by the Allied forces. By the time World War II started, the company's Merlin engines powered Spitfires, Hurricanes, and Lancaster bombers in the skies over Europe and Asia.

Yet Britain's luxury carmaker wasn't the only manufacturer pressed into military service across Europe. French carmaker Renault made crucial contributions to the Allied efforts. Renault

William Durant, cofounder of General Motors, was a pacifist who wanted no involvement with any war machinery production. He refused to allow Cadillac to produce Liberty engines, leading his business partner, Henry Leland, to leave to form Lincoln. Durant later changed his mind, but Lincoln had already received $10 million in government orders.

ROLLS TO RUBIES

Rolls-Royce's armored cars—though used extensively in European wars—might be most recognized in the Middle East. The legendary T. E. Lawrence, an archaeologist and British Army officer, (known as Lawrence of Arabia, as portrayed by Peter O'Toole, pictured above) used them in the Arabian campaigns and notoriously said, "A Rolls in the desert is above rubies."

initially focused on providing cars for the military, and the entire fleet of Renault's Parisian cabs was commandeered for troop transport.

In addition to the vital contribution of Renault's taxi fleet, the company's development of armored tanks provided more military aid. Although not as heavily armed and imposing as the British tanks, the Renault tanks could move faster, and the sheer quantity in production made them an effective weapon. Renault manufactured about 3,600 of the tanks, accounting for more than half of the tanks used by the Allied forces.

World War I inadvertently gave Renault the tools and opportunity it needed to create commercial vehicle offshoots. Using a tank as its inspiration, the company produced its first tractor. Today, Renault has spun most of these sub-divisions off from the car company.

Citroën was a smaller French manufacturer that, before the outbreak of the war, was not a vehicle maker at all, yet was key to the war effort in Europe. The company's engineers developed the double-helix gear pattern that proved vital for Citroën's postwar success as an automaker. During the war, the company converted almost all of its manufacturing plant to munitions and produced weapons for the Allied forces, focusing on vehicles for the first time when the war ended.

Ford made a deep impact on the Allied war effort, particularly in the United Kingdom, converting all of its manufacturing to war machinery. The Model T factories converted to produce ambulances based on its famous design. In the United States, Ford began producing tanks for shipment to the European front, but its M1918 tank was not a success; the US government canceled its contract during the war. The benefit to Ford in the postwar period was enormous, as in the United Kingdom, two in every five vehicles on the road were Fords.

Perhaps the most crucial technological contribution to World War I from the United States was the Liberty L-12 aircraft engine. The new Aircraft Production Board assigned several key engineers to develop an engine superior to anything available in Europe. Elbert Hall of Hall-Scott Motors and Jesse Vincent of the Packard Motor Company designed the initial prototype and delivered the eight-cylinder modular engine to Washington in July 1917. The US Department of War immediately ordered 22,500 Liberty engines but divided the manufacturing contracts between many suppliers. By the end of the conflict, the various plants were turning out some 150 engines daily as the original design was modified and improved.

As in Europe, when World War II broke out in 1939, all American passenger-vehicle production ceased by 1942. The focus shifted to producing military vehicles, which saw orders jump from $4 billion to $10 billion after the attack on Pearl Harbor. All US factories were converted, and new ones, such as Chrysler's Detroit Arsenal Tank Plant, were built. The expansion of weaponry,

aircraft, and military vehicle production provided vast new employment opportunities. Advances in technology, particularly in aviation, benefited the civilian passenger market in the postwar years. Some estimates suggest that from 1942 to 1945, some 6 million weapons, 3 million tanks, and 30,000 aircraft were produced in American vehicle factories.

A considerable amount of preparation was put into the buildup for World War II, particularly in North America and the United Kingdom, where "shadow factories" had already been created on the sites of automotive plants, ready for any potential conflict. The French and German companies were less prepared. In Germany, automakers couldn't fully convert to making weapons and military vehicles, including aircraft, until 1943—despite Ford's German plants being taken over by the Nazi regime. Although the United States continued civilian car production before the attack on Pearl Harbor, the post-attack period eliminated the manufacturing of all passenger vehicles.

While jeeps, tanks, and military trucks were the focus of production, most automotive firms were also involved in producing machine guns, carbines, bombs, and other weaponry. The shadow factories proved a vital decision in the United Kingdom, as American and European factories were slower than expected to convert from car-making. Substantial modifications were needed, and new plants had to be built from scratch in the heart of the American industry in Michigan.

Almost all manufacturers were commandeered for the war effort, including Daimler facilities in the United Kingdom that were converted for war production. Ford's facilities in Germany all came under Nazi control. When Germany invaded and annexed France, all Renault tank manufacture switched from Allied to Nazi control. German automaker Volkswagen was reluctant to involve itself in the war effort, but its output was nationalized by the Nazi regime.

As with World War I, the innovations during World War II were eagerly applied to the passenger-vehicle market when hostilities ended, increasing efficiency and output as well as cementing automakers' role in aircraft engine development.

THE TOP 10 FAMOUS CARS

AFE 495A

1

The General Lee featured in the TV series *The Dukes of Hazzard* is based on a 1969 Dodge Charger. The show's version is known for its stunts, police chases, welded-shut doors (forcing the Dukes to hop in and out through the windows), and signature horn that plays the first 12 notes of the song "Dixie's Land." The car's name is a reference to General Robert E. Lee, and its roof is adorned with the Confederate battle flag.

2

Herbie, the Love Bug, a Volkswagen Beetle, first appeared on screen in *The Love Bug* (1968) and later returned to develop a long-running franchise in movies including *Herbie Rides Again* (1974), *Herbie Goes to Monte Carlo* (1977), and *Herbie Goes Bananas* (1980). Self-driving and seemingly with a will of its own, the car is adept at all sorts of stunts and is adorned with the racing number 53.

3 The Batmobile has undergone many transformations throughout its comic book, television, and cinematic history. The latest model, the Batmobile Tumbler, featured in several *Batman* movies, is more tanklike than some of its predecessors, but it still has such requisite gadgets as the bat deflector and bat radar.

4 KITT, also known as Knight Industries Two Thousand and then later Knight Industries Three Thousand, is an artificially intelligent, self-driving, fully armored car featured in the TV series *Knight Rider,* starring David Hasselhoff (pictured right), and the movie of the same name. Based originally on a Pontiac Trans Am, the later KITT was a Ford Shelby GT500KR.

5 Bessie was a canary-yellow Edwardian roadster driven primarily by the third incarnation of the Doctor in *Doctor Who* during his exile on Earth. Other incarnations of the Doctor have also driven the car. The vintage vehicle was heavily tricked out with many hidden devices, including a super-drive function and remote control. The car's many modifications often confounded the Doctor's enemies.

6 Aston Martin Bondmobile first

appeared in the third movie in the James Bond franchise, *Goldfinger* (1964). The silver-gray Aston Martin DB5 was provided by the British secret service for its Agent 007 to use in the field, complete with an ejector seat, machine guns, armor plating, and satellite navigation. James Bond drove many other vehicles in subsequent films, but the DB5 was clearly his personal favorite, as he retained it throughout the first 50 years of the franchise—until it was completely destroyed in *Skyfall*.

7 Greased Lightnin'

was the subject of a song by the same name in the musical *Grease*. In the movie adaptation, the broken-down car was lovingly restored by the T-Birds gang and used not only to impress the female troupe Pink Ladies, but also to win a close road race through Los Angeles's storm-drain system. At the end of the movie, a bright red version of the car flies the lead characters, Sandy and Danny, off into the sunset, happily ever after.

8 The Ectomobile is a limousine-style ambulance-car in the *Ghostbusters* movies. Broken down and needing "suspension work and shocks, brakes, brake pads, lining, steering box, transmission, rear-end . . . new rings, mufflers, a little wiring," it is adapted for transporting ghost remains by Dan Aykroyd's character, Ray, who puchased the wreck for $4,800.

9 The DeLorean DMC12 was the only car produced by the ill-fated DeLorean Motor Company. In the movie series *Back to the Future*, the modified vehicle is used as a time machine by Marty McFly, having been developed by his inventor friend "Doc" Brown. The vehicle's "flux capacitor" is powered by plutonium that Brown stole from Libyan terrorists.

10 Chitty Chitty Bang Bang is the vintage race car able to fly and float on water in the children's book, film musical, and stage production of the same name. Creator Ian Fleming took his inspiration for the car from a series of racing cars built by Polish-born Count Louis Zborowski in the 1920s, naming it Chitty Bang Bang (later Chitty Chitty Bang Bang) because of the sound the car made when it was started.

THE BIG THREE

DESPITE AN ABUNDANCE OF
AUTOMAKERS IN THE
19TH CENTURY, THREE EMERGED
AS INDUSTRY LEADERS

From the early 1900s, the Big Three automakers—Ford, General Motors, Chrysler—began to dominate the US and global automotive markets, capturing the lion's share of world sales. The companies emerged quickly as the three largest manufacturers, a status they maintained through the 1980s. They remain among the biggest automakers in the new millennium.

The Ford Motor Company was the first of the Big Three to emerge, launched in a converted factory under Ford's stewardship. Ford had already formed the Ford Company in 1901, but in 1902 it became the Cadillac Motor Company, and Ford left to reestablish his own brand. Working with just $28,000 in capital from investors that included future carmakers John and Horace Dodge, Ford organized his workforce into groups for specific tasks of vehicle construction. This method evolved into the assembly-line production that revolutionized the industry within 10 years.

While Ford's company made its start in Dearborn, Michigan, hundreds of miles away in Tarrytown, New York, Jonathan Dixon

A view inside the Ford Motor Company factory with rows of new Model T motor cars.

Maxwell and Benjamin Briscoe founded the Maxwell-Briscoe Company in 1904. A fire destroyed the Tarrytown plant in 1907, and the company moved to Indiana, where the Indianapolis Foundry became the largest automobile factory in the world. By 1914 the company was renamed the Maxwell Company and taken over by Walter Flanders, who decided to move the head-quarters to Detroit.

The Maxwell Company found it hard to compete with the lower-priced Ford, Brush Motor Car Company, Black Car Company, and Oldsmobile, and struggled to stay afloat during World War I. The postwar recession left Maxwell in debt and with much unsold stock. Walter P. Chrysler, a heavy investor in the company, formed a merger with the Chalmers company, and by 1925 took full control, naming his new company Chrysler Corporation.

GM was the third of the Big Three to rise up in the expanding automotive industry. William C. Durant owned McLaughlin Car Company of Canada when he joined forces with Charles Stewart Mott to create General Motors (GM), in Flint, Michigan, in September 1908. GM expanded rapidly, acquiring many carmakers within its first year in operation. By the end of 1909, Oldsmobile, Cadillac, Elmore, Oakland, Reliance, and Rapid had all come under GM's umbrella.

When Durant lost control of GM in 1911, he cofounded the Chevrolet Motor Car Company. However, by 1915 he was back in charge at GM, having secretly bought stock in the company, and incorporated as General Motors Corporation in 1916.

Each of the Big Three companies contributed to the industry's expansion through various innovations, creating three-way competition that benefited consumers, even if their monopoly eradicated smaller competitors by acquiring or outperforming their brands.

Ford introduced the first removable cylinder head as part of the Model T engine in 1908, and the Model A in 1927 featured the first windshield with safety glass. Five years later, a relatively inexpensive V8 engine was included in Ford models.

GM focused on expansion, acquiring Vauxhall Motors in the United Kingdom in 1925 and taking control of 80 percent of German carmaker Opel in 1929. By 1931 GM had full ownership, and the same year GM took over Holden in Australia.

Chrysler focused on creating divisions for its vehicles by class and price. Plymouth was launched to expand into lower-priced markets, whereas DeSoto filled the medium ranges. Dodge and Fargo were purchased to expand in the truck and higher-priced markets, but by the 1930s Dodge and DeSoto switched places in the Chrysler hierarchy. The Imperial line was reserved for the top end of the range, and later spun off independently to compete with Cadillac and Lincoln.

Each of the Big Three pioneered innovations in the postwar period. Chrysler introduced electric fuel injection with its 1958 models. Ford made safety and comfort innovations in the 1950s, including the first dish-style steering wheel, padded dashboards, childproof locks, and rear seatbelts. The first retractable hard roof came at the same time. GM's expansion made it the largest corporation in the United States and the largest employer in the world.

As European carmakers continued to focus on smaller fuel-efficient models, the Big Three followed suit in the 1960s, creating more streamlined vehicles. GM's Chevrolet Corvair was an air-cooled, flat six-cylinder model that competed with the Volkswagen Beetle. Chrysler discontinued the DeSoto brand at the same time, replacing it with the sleeker Valiant, designed to appeal to younger drivers. Meanwhile,

UPWARDLY MOBILE

General Motors's president, Charles Wilson, was made secretary of defense by President Eisenhower in 1953, thanks partly to GM's focus on armaments and air craft engines during World War II.

Ford introduced the Mustang and expanded its overseas models, becoming the largest manufacturer in the United Kingdom by producing the Corsair, Zephyr, and Zodiac ranges, and later the Cortina and Anglia.

Japan and Germany had reemerged as powerhouses by the 1970s, with their vehicle manufacturing industries as their economic backbone. Heavy union restriction in American manufacturing had changed little since the assembly-line process was introduced decades earlier, making it harder for the Big Three to compete outside the United States as more foreign imports made their way into the domestic market.

Meanwhile, GM was challenged in the 1970s when its Vega models struggled to retain market share, as quality issues and labor disputes disrupted production and led to its discontinuation by 1977. At the same time, Oldsmobile began to soar ahead of the competition. The Cutlass series, which included a Rocket V8 engine, became the best-selling car of the decade for any automaker. Overall, Oldsmobile remained third, behind Ford and Chrysler's Chevrolet, in terms of individual brands. As Oldsmobile sales increased, GM was unable to meet production demands and began equipping the Cutlass with the Chevrolet 350 engine. This change was kept from the public, leading to a public-relations disaster and a class-action lawsuit when drivers discovered they were unable to make basic repairs. Parts did not fit, which

[
General Motors diversified to such a degree during the early 2000s that one of its key revenue sources was mortgage loans, particularly in the subprime market. The collapse of the industry cost GM heavily.
]

exposed that they'd been sold an incorrect engine. To restore prestige and limit the damaging fallout, GM began including statements that their models were fitted with standard GM engines, and the GM Powertrain became the name for all GM engines.

The oil crisis of the 1970s and rising gas prices made fuel efficiency a consumer requisite, further pushing Japanese models forward in North American markets. Honda, Nissan, and Toyota made inroads in the US market and elsewhere, while Ford and GM-Vauxhall struggled to compete with German, Italian, and French automakers' fuel-efficient compact models.

In the 1980s, Japanese automakers agreed to import limits, and new technology and lower fuel prices saw the Big Three bounce back. Although Chrysler had been on the verge of bankruptcy in 1979, it came back strongly. It began producing minivans and acquired Jeep, benefiting from the sports utility vehicle (SUV) boom. Ford posted losses in the 1980s of $3.3 billion, but thanks to its Taurus line and efficiency advances, Ford's profit rebounded. GM invested heavily in new technology and diversified its interests beyond auto production, all of which helped the company forge ahead.

Economic recession and changing consumer attitudes in the 1990s again affected the auto industry, but the Big Three were better prepared than before to make market gains, despite the downturn in sales. Each company sold popular vans and SUVs, which ran on diesel and circumvented some of the fuel-efficiency regulations. Millions of pickup trucks were sold, boosting sales dramatically. The acquisition of foreign automakers played a big part in the Big Three's success. GM took control of or made large investments in Saab, Daewoo, Subaru, Hummer, and Fiat. Ford took ownership of Volvo, Jaguar, and Land Rover. Both Ford and GM

Making the bodies for Model T Fords, 1915. Factory workers on the production line completing upholstery for the seats.

invested in Chinese manufacturing, while Japanese and German automakers opened plants in the United States. Chrysler merged with Germany's Daimler-Benz, but turmoil led to the new firm's sale to Cerberus Capital Management, making the company wholly US-owned once more. Oldsmobile and Plymouth were finally discontinued in the first few years of the new millennium, and the pickup trucks and gas-guzzler SUVs, which had been so popular in the 1990s, lost favor as gas prices soared.

Despite streamlining production and embracing new technology, the Big Three have continued to struggle. GM saw significant drops in production, leading to layoffs and plant closures. The cutbacks had a major impact on the Michigan economy, with the city of Detroit filing for bankruptcy. The Big Three's attempts to offer better leasing, zero financing, rebates, and promotional deals have helped maintain sales but have cut deeply into profitability. Light-truck plants have been converted to make smaller energy-efficient vehicles, and huge investments have been made in non-gas-fired engines.

In 2009 GM filed for Chapter 11 bankruptcy, but this did not affect its Canadian or global organization. The move coincided with Chrysler's emergence from Chapter 11 reorganization and its being bought by Italian automaker Fiat (previously under GM control), which technically reduced the US automakers to a Big Two. As of 2014, Fiat owned all of Chrysler. Meanwhile, Ford announced drops in sales and revenue but has continued to remain profitable.

Despite the downturns, American auto manufacturers remain among the most profitable in the world. More than 11 million vehicles were produced in the United States in 2013. As of 2015, General Motors is the third-biggest automaker in the world, behind Toyota and Volkswagen. Ford has fallen back to fifth, and Fiat-Chrysler has fallen to seventh.

Globally recognized brands such as Buick, Cadillac, Chevrolet, Ford, and Lincoln still command significant shares of the US market, whereas the Chrysler name has been rebranded. In December 2014, Fiat-Chrysler was renamed FCA US LLC, ending almost 90 years of an iconic name in global motoring.

OF BANKRUPTCY AND BAILOUTS

WHAT HAPPENS WHEN THE AUTO MARKET FALLS?

Although the automobile industry has been rocked by financial issues many times—during the Great Depression, the 1970s oil crisis, the early-1980s economic woes, and the 1990s recession—the global recession in 2008 proved especially detrimental to the automotive sector.

The problems in the United States were accentuated by years of declining sales and the rising popularity of imported vehicles. Severe credit restrictions also hampered sales. By 2009 the American auto industry was in desperate crisis.

To combat the alarming decline, the Big Three—Ford, General Motors, Chrysler—applied for short-term emergency loans, but by April 2009 GM and Chrysler were in danger of liquidation. Within a year, both companies had filed for Chapter 11 bankruptcy, after the US government and its Canadian counterpart approved $85 billion in an effort to stave off mass layoffs.

The measures were highly criticized. At first, the US Congress rejected the bailout plans. Just as GM closed 20 factories and Chrysler suspended 30 plants, the Senate refused to pass the package in December 2008. Eventually, after aspects of the bill were revised, the Emergency Economic Stabilization Act of 2008 was signed into law by President George W. Bush, and $17.5 billion was released to both GM and Chrysler. The same month, the two companies appealed to Congress again for an additional $22 billion, which was approved by incoming President Barack Obama—with a package of job cuts and GM's sale of its Swedish brand, Saab, as part of the deal.

GM and Chrysler restructured their massive debts and emerged from protection, but as a result GM was technically owned by the US Treasury, whereas Chrysler was in the joint hands of Italy's Fiat and the United Auto Workers union. Although GM and Chrysler survived, many of their brands were discontinued, and hundreds of dealerships were terminated.

The Ford Motor Company, the oldest of the Big Three, remained intact and never faced bankruptcy proceedings, thanks in part to a significant line of credit obtained in 2007.

POPULAR MEASURES

As a result of rebounding sales and production, a majority of Americans saw the bailout as useful to the US economy, according to public opinion polls conducted in 2012 by Pew Research. A vocal minority of Americans dissented, however, leading to a backlash in public opinion against government bailouts of automakers as well as Wall Street.

The biggest challenge facing the Big Three was a lack of access to offshore manufacturing that was enjoyed by their foreign counterparts. The companies blamed restrictive labor practices for stifling flexibility and profitability, something felt less deeply by other makers, which had shifted production to Mexico, Brazil, and China.

The global recession that plagued all aspects of the world economy was perhaps compounded by the early-2000s energy crisis. The automakers' reliance on truck and SUV sales in the 1990s led to high inventory for autos now falling out of fashion. Japanese, German, French, Italian, and Korean automakers were focusing on smaller energy-efficient vehicles and were somewhat shielded from the severe crisis facing the Big Three.

Despite the turmoil, the Big Three returned to profit and increased sales of their newer, more popular lines. In 2011 GM's North American sales were ahead of Toyota's, reaching more than 9 million units, although the US government was forced to write off about $14 billion of its bailout loans.

Although the companies survived in various forms, the industry itself was transformed. Workers' concessions to reduced conditions and benefits were in place, and Michigan—Detroit especially—was economically decimated, as production was shifted elsewhere. The Center for Automotive Research reported that for every auto-sector job created by a foreign company, 6.1 jobs were lost by the Big Three.

Had the bailouts and restructuring not taken place, an estimated 3 million jobs could have been lost, the companies claimed, with an economic impact of about $400 billion hitting the US economy over three years. The loss in tax revenue and the need to pay welfare benefits could have cost the government an estimated $156 billion. The loss of any one of the Big Three would have meant an additional 1 million vehicles imported from foreign brands, costing the domestic economy a projected $25 billion.

Many people feared that too much government intervention would send the car industry into the same tailspin that the United Kingdom had felt in the 1970s. There, the failing British Leyland had been nationalized, and parts of the corporation were jettisoned to focus on the Rover and Austin brands. All aspects of the British car industry came under foreign owner-ship, and even highly respected brands like Range Rover, Jaguar, and Mini are now owned by overseas companies—a situation that the US government was desperate to avoid. Fiat's takeover of Chrysler is seen by many as the first step in this inevitable process.

CAR TALK
HOSTED BY BROTHERS
TOM AND RAY MAGLIOZZI

Car Talk was the highly popular weekly radio show hosted by brothers Tom and Ray Magliozzi, both MIT graduates, who styled themselves "Click and Clack, the Tappet Brothers," on WBUR-FM in 1977, and syndicated nationally from 1987 through 2012.

The premise of the hour-long show was that listeners would call in and describe their challenges with malfunctioning vehicles. A huge part of the show's success derived from callers recreating sound effects to describe their cars' or trucks' problems, while the two brothers attempted to diagnose the issue.

The hosts' easygoing nature and straight-talking style earned popularity beyond the National Public Radio (NPR) network. The brothers' casual, unrehearsed banter with their interactive audience earned the program its official slogan: "Unencumbered by the thought process."

Callers were encouraged to dial what became an internationally recognized phone number, 1-800-CAR-TALK, and as many as 2,000 calls would be received by the production team every week. As the show's slogan suggested, the hosts were never briefed on what callers would ask, nor were the callers briefed on anything but basic technical issues of being on radio via telephone. The best calls recorded were retained for the final weekly broadcast.

Other features of the show, which expanded from its original two segments to three (jokingly referred to by the hosts as the "third half"), included the weekly "Puzzler," in which a challenge would be set for listeners to send in answers about a rare and usually nonexistent item such as a $26 bill. Highlights also included the "Puzzler Towers," in which the winner would win a gift certificate for the *Car Talk* store, known as the Shameless Commerce Division. "Stump the Chumps" followed an earlier slot called "Where Are They Now, Tommy?," which had begun in 1981. Return callers were invited to share the success or failure of the hosts' advice.

A recurring guest of the Tappet Brothers was their "animal-vehicle biologist and wildlife guru," Kieran Lindsey, who answered questions for drivers living in less-urban areas. One question she received became a running joke on the show: "How do I remove a snake from my car?"

Celebrity guests were occasionally featured, including Geena Davis, Ashley Judd, and Martha Stewart. Infamously, the brothers twice referred to Stewart as "Margaret" during the broadcast. In 1992, the show won a Peabody Award, which cited the show as a weekly "mental tune-up" for radio listeners.

Outside of their broadcast world, the Magliozzi brothers owned and ran a garage together in Harvard Square in Cambridge, Massachusetts, the home of their broadcasts. The program's corporate office was named after the show's imaginary lawyers—Dewey, Cheetham, and Howe (pronounced "Do we cheat 'em, and how").

The show was spun off into a short-lived animated series for PBS in 2008, and it inspired the 1995 sitcom *The George Wendt Show*. In 2011 *Car Talk: The Musical!!!* opened in Boston.

Ill health forced Tom Magliozzi to relinquish the show, and the brothers retired in 2012, although reruns of the show continue across NPR. Tom Magliozzi died on November 3, 2014, of complications from Alzheimer's, yet the show lives on with enormous popularity.

FORD
UNFAIR TO
United Auto Workers
Local 325
STRIKE ON
UNFAIR TO
United Auto Workers
LOCAL 325
FORD

THE STATE OF THE UNION

FROM FORD'S ANTI-UNION THUGS TO TODAY'S UAW

The International Union, United Automobile, Aerospace and Agricultural Implement Workers of America (UAW) has been an integral part of the North American motor industry since the 1930s. Membership spans the United States, Canada, and Puerto Rico.

Founded as part of the Congress of Industrial Organizations (CIO), the union and its influence increased rapidly, playing a key part in American politics, the civil rights movement, and the fight against communism in the United States.

Industrial unions were created in 1935 in the heart of the Motor City, Detroit, as part of the American Federation of Labor (AFL), which had represented more craft-sector workers than factory workers. The unions soon splintered from AFL and CIO, led by John Lewis and a number of labor activists.

Left: February 1937, United Auto Workers Union members picket the Ford plant in St. Louis, MO.

Almost immediately, the fledgling UAW was in contention with auto executives as the union began a sit-down strike in General Motors's Atlanta plant in 1936, which led to the more famous protest in Flint, Michigan, in December 1936. The strike lasted almost two months and was extremely damaging to GM. Only the intervention of Michigan's governor brought a resolution, which led to GM recognizing the union, as did Chrysler the following month.

With the UAW established in two of the Big Three, it focused next on the Ford Motor Company, which had resolutely refused its employees' attempts to unionize. Henry Ford's manager and security director, Harry Bennett, a former boxing champion, used brute force to quell any attempts to bring unionized labor to the Ford workplace. Under Ford's new Service Department, he used intimidation and internal surveillance to enforce Henry Ford's vision of a union-free environment. Violence erupted several times between employees and the Service Department, and between Bennett and union leaders themselves, leading to the very ugly Battle of the Overpass on May 26, 1937. Initially, the UAW had planned to issue a leaflet titled "Unionism, Not Ford-ism" to workers at a pedestrian overpass near the River Rouge Plant complex in Dearborn, Michigan. Among the demands

James E. (Scotty) Kilpatrick, a photographer for *Detroit News*, was on hand to document the union organizers at the infamous Battle of the Overpass. While other photographers had their plates and cameras destroyed, Kilpatrick managed to outsmart Harry Bennett and his men. His powerful images spread the story across the country and inspired the administrators of the Pulitzer Prize to institute an award for photography.

were six-hour workdays and an increase in wages from $6 to $8 (equivalent to $131 today).

The incident turned vicious when UAW leaders were attacked from behind and beaten by Bennett's department as the workers attempted to pose for news photographs. The skirmish spread to more than 40 people in which at least 16 were injured.

Many of the injuries were severe. Management claimed that the workers had provoked the conflict, despite photographic evidence.

It took considerably more time and violence between Ford and the UAW before the union gained recognition in the company. In 1941, Ford finally agreed to collective bargaining.

One of Ford's many fears had been the infiltration of communists into the union. However, Ford's concessions to allow full recognition for the UAW brought a less-confrontational attitude from the union, which recognized that its strikes and disruptions were strains on the union and its members as much as on Ford.

World War II had a deep impact on the UAW's relationship with auto executives,

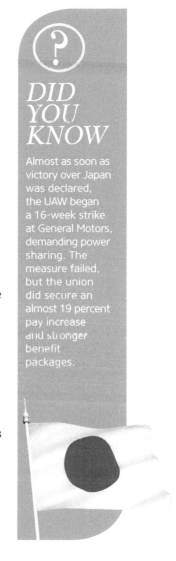

and although many of its leaders disagreed, the union adopted a no-strike pledge for the duration of the war. At the same time, the UAW expanded, unionizing workers at cycle manufacturing plants.

UAW membership grew steadily, with its leader, Walter Reuther, overseeing the union's most powerful periods in labor history. His death in 1970 came at the start of a tumultuous period in labor relations and the auto industry.

Changes in the global economy encouraged competition from Japanese and European automakers, as they opened manufacturing plants in the United States, mainly in nonunion areas of the South.

The 1973 oil crisis led to a massive downturn in the fortunes of all American automakers, primarily the heavily unionized Big Three. The UAW was faced with harsh realities of falling demand for American-made cars. The union agreed to layoffs and was pressured to sign away many of the worker benefits it had devoted years to creating.

When Chrysler almost went bankrupt in 1979, the UAW agreed to tighter labor restrictions in the hope of keeping the company alive. By the 1980s the economic landscape was extremely different. When the UAW's Canadian division entered into a protracted dispute, the Canadians broke away from the union to form the Canadian Auto Workers independently, as they felt that only American workers were benefiting from the UAW. This splintering affected the already falling membership of the main union. Estimated membership was 1.5 million in 1979, but by 2006 the number had fallen to about 540,000.

For all its historic battles with the auto corporations, and the criticism that the UAW has received, the union has been widely credited with helping both Chrysler and General Motors survive bankruptcy and remain viable, even with Chrysler under Fiat's ownership.

According to *New York Times* reporting in 2008, entry-level pay rates for UAW workers are lower than those earned by nonunion labor. The creation of a jobs bank program and the suspension of high-level redundancy packages were key concessions by the UAW in helping the companies gain a competitive edge after the global recession.

The UAW has successfully unionized employees outside the Big Three as well. In 2010, the German, Japanese, and Korean plants on US soil were targeted for UAW expansion. In 2014, the Volkswagen plant in Chattanooga, Tennessee, rejected the union, although Volkswagen implemented a policy allowing groups representing at least 15 percent of its workforce to participate in meetings.

Today, UAW members work in industries as diverse as auto production, health care, casino gambling, and higher education. The union has about 390,000 active members and more than 600,000 retired members in 750 local chapters.

A DEEP DIVE IN DETROIT

WHAT IS MOTOR CITY?

Michigan's largest city, Detroit, a.k.a. Motor City, grew out of a fur-trading post settled in 1701 to become the industrial heartland of the United States. The city is recognized as the world's car capital.

By the end of the 19th century, Detroit had already built its economy around the coach and machine industries, so when entrepreneur Henry Ford, from Dearborn, was looking for a base to build his automobile empire, he didn't have to look very far to establish his first factory, at Highland Park. Ford's Piquette Plant opened in 1904, and the area was soon a thriving industrial center. By 1906 the Studebaker plant had opened nearby, after the Cadillac factory's opening in the New Amsterdam district in 1905.

The city expanded as car manufacturing and assembly grew, with larger commercial and office buildings created by Ford, and General Motors's arrival in the 1920s, along with its associated research laboratory.

As auto-making grew, so did Detroit's workforce and population. By 1930 more than 1.5 million people lived and worked in the metropolitan area, up from just 280,000 at the start of the 20th century. Many immigrants from Europe boosted the numbers, and desirable new housing developments sprung up to cope with the population boom created by the auto industry.

Detroit's infrastructure improved, meeting the the city's growing needs. New railroads and bridges were built in the 1920s, expanding the reach of the downtown areas to the suburbs and

DID YOU KNOW

Hudson's downtown department store, the nation's second largest, moved from its city-center location in 1964 to the largest suburban shopping mall in the world to accommodate customers' need for parking facilities.

THE WAR EFFORT

One year prior to the attack on Pearl Harbor, Franklin D. Roosevelt uttered the slogan, "Arsenal of Democracy"— "a call to arm and support" the Allies through the collective efforts of American industry. Roosevelt's economic principle was exemplified by Detroit's production hub, a key part of the Allied war effort.

easing the traffic buildup that was becoming common.

World War II brought further expansion to Detroit, which, despite the war's toll, saw rising levels of employment. With car production suspended, the Big Three's plants were converted to aircraft-engine development in addition to tanks, jeeps, and armaments.

The war also brought many challenges to Detroit, including housing shortages created by the influx of thousands of workers and their families, keen to reap the benefits of the high-paying jobs. In June 1943 tensions erupted into conflicts among various racial groups, and several days of fighting on Detroit's streets led to many deaths, the destruction of property, and hundreds of injured residents. The Army was brought in to restore order.

The postwar economy and the automobile industry's growth saw Detroit enjoying its most prosperous period, leading up to the 1970s. New expressways had been built to facilitate the transportation of goods for the war effort, and new highways were constructed to cope with commuter demands in the early 1950s.

The increase in car ownership and the strengthening of Detroit's roads were detrimental to the public transit systems that had been developed in the 1930s. The city's electric streetcars became redundant, and they were eventually sold to Mexico—a shortsighted decision that many protested.

Racial tensions continued in Detroit, particularly as African-American workers joined the automobile companies in a climate of heated racism in Detroit, a stronghold of highly public white-supremacist groups at the time. By 1960, about 16 percent of workers were black, but as they were employed mainly in entry-level positions, they were vulnerable to layoffs through increased automation and economic fluctuations.

Largely because of the influence of the United Auto Workers union, state and civil rights legislation encouraged the development of a large black middle class, who, like their white counterparts, expanded into homes in the suburbs, escaping downtown housing.

Detroit's urbanization left little room for automakers' plant expansion. New factories could only realistically be built in the suburbs, where wealthy and influential white Detroit families used their political clout to halt automakers' expansion in their neighborhoods.

By the 1970s threats from the global energy crisis—and the growing popularity of German and Japanese vehicles   took

The burgeoning African-American population on Detroit's auto production lines also expanded into pop music in the 1950s, when Motown Records founded its headquarters in the city. "The sound of Motown" carried black artists from Detroit to the top of the world's music charts.

a heavy toll on Detroit, marking the start of its decline. While autoworkers lived in the expanding neighborhoods close to out-of-town factories, the center of Detroit became notorious for drugs and violence.

As auto manufacturing shed hundreds of thousands of jobs, the Detroit area has been deeply challenged in the 21st century. Concerted efforts to revitalize the city center have struggled to gain momentum as economic woes have engulfed the city. Chapter 11 bankruptcies for Chrysler and General Motors caused rocketing unemployment, with Ford cutting many jobs as it fought to remain solvent. In July 2013, the city announced that it would default on its $18 billion debt and declared bankruptcy—the biggest municipal bankruptcy in U.S. history. The road to revival may be long and challenging for Motor City, but as the city's motto proclaims, "We hope for better things; it shall rise from the ashes."

WOMAN DRIVER

THE FIRST ECO-FRIENDLY
RACE CAR DRIVER

Leilani Maaja Münter is an American race-car driver, Tesla-brand enthusiast, and onetime body double for actress Catherine Zeta-Jones. Münter drives in the ARCA Racing Series, having previously competed in the Firestone Indy Lights

Münter made her racing debut in the Allison Legacy Series in 2001, before switching to NASCAR the following year, competing in Mooresville, North Carolina, and then at south Boston Speedway and Texas Motor Speedway. She has set records for female drivers along the way. She became the first woman ever to qualify for the Tony Bettenhausen Memorial Classic in Indiana and was repeatedly a top-five finisher in stock-car racing. By 2007 she qualified for the ARCA Series, in Daytona, but she took an offer from the IndyCar team for open-wheel racing. A year later she made a stock-car appearance at Daytona, driving for Mark Gibson Racing.

As only the fourth woman to complete the IndyPro Series, Münter is highly accomplished. Unfortunately, she was involved in a multi-car collision in her Kentucky Speedway debut in August 2007, while sitting in fourth place. It knocked her out of the contest, though many top drivers, including Rick Mears and Jaques Lazier, spoke highly of her debut.

Together with Danica Patrick and Alli Owens, Münter is one of the three most recognizable women in racing history. The three have often been the only women on the starting grid in the ARCA Racing Series. By 2014, Münter was driving for Venturini Motorsports in the ARCA series, and she competed at Daytona in the number 55 "Go 100% Renewable Energy" car. Though she spun out of the race in a wreck, she has finished several other races in eco-sustainable vehicles. *Sports Illustrated* named her one of the world's top-10 female drivers, while *Glamour* magazine credited her as an "eco hero." Other awards followed from *Elle* magazine, which gave her its Genius Award. Her product endorsements have included Lucky Brand Jeans and Hostess, which featured her alongside Danica Patrick as well as racer Melanie Troxel.

Münter's eco-activism has earned her global recognition. She decried the Gulf of Mexico oil spill in 2010. Her blogging and activism have taken her to Washington to speak out at environmental issues and earned her Discovery Channel's Planet Green Network's Number-One Eco-Athlete in the World award.

In 2013 Münter purchased a P85+ Tesla Motors Model S and took on state legislators who had introduced a bill to ban Tesla sales in North Carolina. Tesla CEO Elon Musk has been a strong supporter of Münter and has invited her to speak at many events. Münter charges her Tesla vehicle using solar panels on the roof of her North Carolina home.

SPRAWL FOR ALL

WITH CARS COME SUBURBS

Although suburban expansion had begun by the late 19th century, the rush for Americans to live outside major city centers accelerated in the second half of the 20th century, following World War II.

As American cities had developed, everything existed side by side, regardless of function. This led to the phrase "walking cities"—residences, shops, schools, medical facilities, and other

[
Despite road and suburban development, only 17 percent of the nation's population lived in suburbia in 1920, and the slow development continued. By 1940 the number was only 20 percent, due largely to the Great Depression.
]

spaces jostled for position, sometimes sharing the same building. These "walking cities" were congested, partly because of narrow streets, with horses and carriages unable to negotiate the terrain.

The earliest suburbs were designated by city governments for tasks and businesses like slaughterhouses, soap manufacturing, and tanneries—whereas homeless camps and homes for urban workers developed unfettered. Gradually, wealthier residents looked beyond city centers for areas less bustling and stressful. As long as the city center remained within reach, the growing number of wealthy residents were happy to seek quieter refuge and enjoy a more country-style life.

The post–World War I period saw an economic boom that pioneered motoring. Paved roads led to the suburbs, creating a freeway system that fed both metropolitan sprawl and urban deterioration. The automobile became the number-one consideration for all urban planning.

The great suburban expansion came after World War II. Postwar legislation to benefit returning veterans created an educated workforce with access to better housing. The new professional classes in the United States, and veterans who chose vocational education, beefed up the service sector. Both groups began having children who would become "baby boomers," and they needed low-cost housing. Despite the federal backing of home loans, a housing shortage proved an obstacle. The suburbs provided a clear solution.

The postwar period saw Americans buying cars in unprecedented numbers. Some 70,000 cars were sold by the end of 1945, with that number increasing to more than 2 million in 1946, and more than 5 million by 1949. Many American families not only bought their first cars but also a second. The emergence of two-car families made suburbia even more attractive, as one spouse could take a car into the city or other commercial area while the second vehicle remained at home for shuttling children to school and for running errands.

The car's mark on the land reached well beyond cities and their immediate surroundings. Expressways accelerated movement, especially with the construction of superhighways and the interstate system. The National Interstate and Defense Highways Act of 1956 committed the nation to a coast-to-coast toll-free system with greater dependence on automobile travel than ever before. The Highway Trust Fund was established to finance the system, drawing revenue from taxes on fuel, truck use, and tire sales. It also undermined any federally sponsored mass-transit programs.

Retail outlets and shopping areas became automobile-friendly. The appearance of shopping malls with ample parking represented a commitment to motorized traffic, providing a concentration of stores only accessible by vehicles. The earliest shopping centers outside central business districts were built in the 1920s, such as the shopping district in the suburbs of Kansas City. There were only eight of these centers in the country by the end of World War II. By 1960, the number had risen to an astonishing 4,000. Today, cars are as much a part of the urban landscape as the buildings they shuttle passengers among.

STATUS SIGN OF THE TIMES

HOW EGO AND IDENTITY ARE EMBODIED ON THE ROAD

The automobile has been one of the most powerful status symbols in American culture and society since the early 20th century. From its earliest days, one of General Motors's goals was for vehicles to become status symbols that illustrated a defined social-class structure. The concept was to encourage consumers to spend money on luxury goods that power. By offering various makes and models, the company

provided different levels of social status to meet the demands of consumers who wanted to display wealth.

Ford and General Motors each had a strong impact on social status. Henry Ford's focus was one car, one color, all for one price. Ford's vision was not only to manufacture a product for the masses, but by pioneering the $5 daily wage, he created a market for his product. Ford's strategy chipped away at the social status and exclusivity that went with owning a car. Ford's contrast to General Motors was stark. General Motors catered to people looking to gain status through individualism with various makes, models, and finishes.

Status had become a key marketing tool for all the automakers by the late 1920s. It wasn't enough to be satisfied with just having a car; it had to be the newer, more expensive model that everyone desired. Advertising campaigns played heavily into this psyche.

The car became the ideal way for Americans to display wealth and indicate that they had "made it." In many respects, the car even replaced the home as the most important status symbol. Luxury carmakers began to thrive alongside the Big Three, particularly in Europe, where Bentleys and Rolls-Royces became an almost unattainable dream for most motorists.

Mass-produced cars and the luxury vehicle market diversified further in the 1930s. General Motors offered the basic Chevrolet, the more expensive and desirable Pontiac, the middle-range

Imported vehicles such as the Volkswagen Beetle and Minibus also thrived, but were seen as "anti-status symbols" favored by the baby-boomer generation eschewing the rapid rise of consumerism.

Oldsmobile and Buick, and the top-level Cadillac. Chrysler also offered a range of models aimed at creating a tiered status market. The Dodge, Plymouth, and Chrysler lines were all developed in specific price and comfort ranges, with the luxurious New Yorker topping the fleet. Ford's basic model progressed to the higher-level Mercury, and the elite Lincoln Continental aimed at the most affluent buyers.

New technology and engineering, as well as "extras," fed the consumer desire for bigger and better. The models were targeted as either family-friendly, sporty, sturdy, or luxurious. The black Model T that had been so successful was no longer acceptable to buyers who wanted various colors of vehicles to distinguish themselves from neighbors who may have the same model.

The post-World War II period saw big surges in car ownership, as owning multiple vehicles became as much a symbol of success as the model itself. In Europe, BMW, Mercedes-Benz, Ferrari, Aston Martin, and Porsche were developing extremely expensive luxury models desired by wealthy Americans who wished to set themselves apart visibly.

COMMON PROBLEM

One of the challenges facing Ford's mass-market approach was that the Model T lost its cachet once many people had one. Despite being cheaper and more reliable, Fords were surpassed in sales by the wider variety and unique models offered by General Motors.

American manufacturers began to create sleeker, faster, more stylish models to attract younger drivers. The "muscle car" was born in the 1960s; Ford led the way with the introduction of the Mustang. The Pontiac GTO and Chevy Camaro soon followed and became iconic with younger generations.

The oil crisis of the 1970s saw a big shift in the way American consumers viewed vehicles. Europeans had long favored smaller energy-efficient models, whereas size was an indicator of status for American drivers. As most American manufacturers—particularly the Big Three—focused on big cars with big engines, smaller Japanese and German models became more popular. American automakers had the makings of a public-relations disaster as foreign vehicles became symbols of reliability and efficiency.

1985 Ferrari 288 GTO

The increase in young, wealthy, single Americans in the 1980s—the yuppie generation—pushed for a power vehicle to match the power suit. The development of the sport utility vehicle in the 1990s was unprecedented, as size once again became more important than fuel efficiency for nonfamily drivers. The 21st century has witnessed a shift in desireability toward eco-friendly options, from the Prius to the Tesla.

The automobile remains perhaps the most powerful status symbol of the past century. What started as a novelty for the very wealthy is now common transportation that fits every niche of almost every status level.

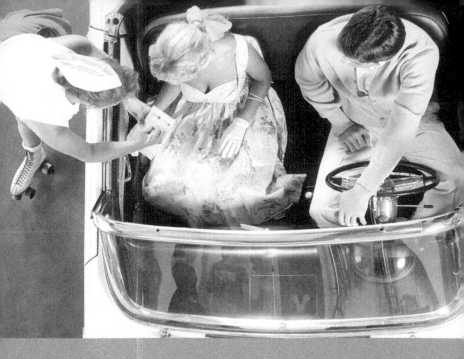

THE FASTEST FOODS

THE DESTINATION RESTAURANT OF THE 1950s: THE FRONT SEAT

Fast food began to gain popularity in the 1920s, famously spearheaded by Patrick McDonald, who opened a food stand known as the Airdrome in Monrovia, California, in 1937, selling burgers for 10 cents and juices for 5 cents.

His two sons, Richard and Maurice, who worked as film grips in Hollywood, saw the potential, so they opened a more traditional restaurant in San Bernardino—the McDonald's Bar-B-Q, which flourished. By 1948 the brothers had streamlined a simple, inexpensive menu that was hugely popular.

The brothers began to franchise their restaurant, and by the 1950s many outlets had opened, with the iconic Golden Arches becoming a familiar sight across Southern California, selling burgers, fries, and milk shakes.

A traveling salesman, Chicago-based Ray Kroc of the milk shake-making Multi-Mixer company, was intrigued that his products were widely used by the fledgling McDonald's chain, and he helped develop a plan to pioneer a uniform recipe and a national franchise operation.

Kroc opened the first franchise in Des Plaines, Illinois, near Chicago, and by the early 1960s he'd assumed full control of what became the McDonald's Corporation.

The growth of the automobile was integral to the corporation's success, as suburbanization spread across the United States. Highway expansion meant huge opportunities for fast, affordable food outlets. "Grabbing something to eat" became a literal opportunity thanks to the car.

Drive-in restaurants sprung up in the 1950s to match the increase in car ownership. McDonald's personified the fast-food ethos, as none of its outlets offered seating until 1962, but Kroc took it to a new level by creating drive-through windows to order and collect food almost without stopping the vehicle.

The business model pioneered by Kroc is now global and imitated by many others. The drive-through window is a standard feature of many global fast-food chains.

BIGGER, BETTER?

THE LASTING EFFECTS OF OIL-GUZZLERS

Perhaps in reaction to the prevalence of smaller cars from Japan and Europe, a new breed of rugged vehicles became hugely popular in the 1990s, particularly in the US market. Especially desirable among younger drivers and families, sport utility vehicles (SUVs) did much to regenerate the American auto industry after years of decline.

The designs and engine technology were hardly new. Military vehicles and commercial successes such as Land Rover and Jeep had been around a long time. The styles and engine designs became popular with drivers and manufacturers alike. The new fleet of trucks, minivans, and the other vehicles classified as SUVs were sold and designated as work vehicles rather than simply passenger cars. The term "SUV" is now generally used for any vehicle with four-wheel drive and raised ground clearance. In many countries, an SUV is called a 4WD (four-wheel drive).

The United States was not the only nation to embrace the more rugged and hard-wearing fleets. People in India, Canada, Australia, and the United Kingdom embraced the idea of driving in something better suited for off-road use. The sturdy appearance and larger dimension also gave the impression of improved safety, although because safety standards were already fairly uniform across all model classes of automobiles, this gain was largely imagined.

From the automakers' perspective, the success and popularity of this new sector of motoring were a godsend. The new designs were far cheaper to manufacture, and the margins on similarly priced cars were tiny by comparison. The Big Three manufacturers switched a big portion of their production to passenger trucks and SUVs. Nonetheless, in the longer term, these production decisions may have been harmful, as many of the Big Three's long-running brands fell behind in features, image, and sales. Many were discontinued altogether.

Part of the draw for consumers was the larger cabin, which integrated passenger and cargo space into one. The SUV and minivan could accommodate three rows of seating, which could easily be removed or reconfigured to provide considerable cargo space, as opposed to the traditional trunk. The higher ground clearance was useful in colder climates, as was the four-wheel drive system. Smaller Jeeps, their copycats, and flatbed trucks became immensely popular with younger Americans, and

In 2005 the United States consumed 20.8 million barrels of gasoline every day. Transportation accounted for almost 70 percent of that figure. In total, nearly 25 percent of the world's entire gasoline production is consumed by the United States.

SUVs and minivans were especially preferred by parents.

The expansion of the market and the success of the Big Three in reclaiming lost sales to foreign competitors were significant, yet it all came with challenges. Higher oil prices caused problems in the mid-2000s, and large gas-guzzling vehicles suddenly lost their luster. Higher gas prices saw the revival of smaller energy-efficient vehicles once more, yet the focus on the larger fleets made it hard for American automakers to catch up and compete.

The 2008 global recession hit the North American market even harder, and several plants closed, including many that had been entirely focused on SUV models.

Although drivers are marginally safer in larger, heavier vehicles, there are many safety concerns. Rollover is a bigger problem than in standard-design cars, and improvements in rollover safety have been a focus for carmakers.

Passengers are often given far less protection in a collision because the truck-style chassis is separate from the body of the vehicle. In some fatalities, automakers opted to quietly settle lawsuits brought by victims' families rather than possibly damaging the companies' reputations and sales.

MILITARY MIGHT

Some 55,000 Humvee vehicles were purchased by the US Armed Forces by 1985, a deal worth $1.2 billion to American Motors. The first civilian model was the M998, sold in 1992 under the brand name Hummer.

A driver in Gorham, Maine, fills the tank of her Hummer in 2005, three years before GM would first attempt to sell the brand.

The term gas guzzler became synonymous with larger SUVs, particularly brands such as Hummer, which had been developed for the US Army in the 1970s as a military vehicle that could cover ordinarily inaccessible terrain. As a vehicle for the average motorist, its high gas consumption didn't initially faze those excited to own a quasi-tank. Yet as oil prices rose steadily, the cost of running such a machine escalated. Although very popular at first, the Hummer was discontinued by General Motors as part of the company's bankruptcy reorganization.

The upturn in gas use significantly exacerbated environmental challenges. SUVs, minivans, and trucks generally are less fuel efficient and are not required to meet the minimum levels set for standard cars. Technically classified as light trucks, the vehicles have a minimum fuel requirement of only 20.7 miles per gallon, as opposed to the minimum 27.5 miles per gallon for a standard car.

The design compounds the issue of fuel consumption, as larger mass means increased wind resistance, heavier suspension, and larger drivetrains, making the vehicles less economical to operate. Fuel use has created serious concerns about atmospheric pollutants, as more greenhouse gases and carcinogens are produced by those vehicles in comparison to standard family vehicles.

SUV drivers and dealerships have been targeted by eco-activist groups over fuel use and atmospheric pollution. Some drivers have found their vehicles damaged, others destroyed. In some countries, most notably Sweden, activists have spent considerable effort releasing air from the tires of hundreds of SUVs.

The US Environmental Protection Agency (EPA) recognized the pollution problem and in 2009 mandated that emissions from light trucks and passenger cars become standardized. Yet critics were quick to point out that the EPA's actions came after the dramatic fall in the vehicle's popularity. The damage was already done.

Other studies have focused not just on fuel consumption but on the "dust-to-dust" impact—the complete impact environmentally of a vehicle from its creation to destruction. Some of these studies concluded that 80 percent of any vehicle's environmental impact comes in its manufacture, and that the actual use accounts for only 20 percent. This has been hotly debated by academics and the carmakers.

The environmental impact of Americans' seemingly endless desire for bigger cars has been just one cause for concern over the past few decades. Perhaps a greater worry for the US government is the craving for oil and gasoline from beyond American shores, as domestic demand has always exceeded production. As a consequence, American reliance on imported oil has played a significant part in foreign relations, particularly concerning the Middle East.

In reality, the biggest oil supplier to the United States is its northern neighbor, Canada. However, so much of the world relies on nations in the Middle East, that agreements after World War II by Western nations—the Red Line Agreement and the Anglo-American Petroleum Agreement—have heavily influenced attitudes toward them. Such agreements strictly protected US oil interests in the Middle East and ultimately gave control of international oil prices to American companies in the postwar period.

Arab unrest and resentment toward colonial powers such as Britain and France caused enormous challenges for the imperial overseers. Recognizing its importance, the United States took keen interest in the region. The three pillars of postwar American foreign policy—the Soviet Union, Israel, and access to oil—caused what scholars see as "the great divide" for the United States and Middle East nations.

Egypt's seizure of the Suez Canal from the British was one of the first postwar conflagrations, having the net result of empowering the United States and supplanting the United Kingdom as the dominant power in the region. At least 25 percent of the world's oil supplies travel through its waters, giving the United States ample incentive to intervene.

Subsequent armed conflicts in the region, such as the first and second Gulf wars, have ostensibly been about terrorism and the protection of innocent civilians from murderous rulers, but many observers cite protecting the massive oil reserves in the region as the main goal of thwarting dictators with no allegiance or friendship toward the United States.

The US government's goal of energy independence has been a mantra of all recent administrations, yet American society's relentless demand for gasoline has not made the goal achievable. Today, the United States produces about 60 percent of the gasoline it needs, with the remainder imported from Canada, Saudi Arabia, Mexico, Venezuela, and Russia. This is a big switch from 2005, when 60 percent needed to be imported.

Increasing supplies, mass-transit improvements, rising fuel consumption minimums, and alternative energy sources have helped rebalance the need for oil imports, but there is still a long way to go.

A NOD
TO NADER

IF YOU WEAR A SEATBELT, YOU HAVE RALPH TO THANK

Published in 1965, *Unsafe at Any Speed: The Designed-In Dangers of the American Automobile*, written by Ralph Nader, had a profound impact on the global automobile industry and is seen as a pioneering work.

The book took aim at a number of manufacturing issues, most often directly related to cost cutting. In Chapter 1, "The Sporty Corvair—The One Car Accident", Nader notoriously criticized the early models of the rear-engined Chevrolet Corvair for being at risk of tuck-under crashes. According to Nader, the omission of a front stabilizer (a cost-cutting measure), led to incorrect tire pressures and created dangerous over-steering. In another argument, Nader claimed that crash-testing science had been neglected to make lighter, streamlined models rather than heavier, protective shells. The "Nader bolt," a direct consequence of the book, was introduced to reinforce doors. Nader railed against the engineers who refused to focus on road safety so as not to alienate buyers or make cars more expensive by including safety enhancements. His argument hinged on the assertion that safety features would add just 23 cents to the cost of each car, whereas the design flourishes cost $700.

The impact of Nader's research and arguments has been long lasting, and not just within the United States. In the 1960s the British government mandated that all cars feature passenger safety belts, although the use of seatbelts wasn't enforced by law until 1983. The fitting of air bags also became standard.

The Big Three automakers responded viciously to Nader's book, and Nader claimed that General Motors was trying to ruin his reputation to silence him. General Motors president James Roche was summoned to a Senate committee hearing accusing him of harassment and intimidation against Nader, forcing Roche to apologize publicly in 1966. Another General Motors executive, John DeLorean, broke ranks to publicly admit that most of Nader's arguments were correct.

HYBRIDS, ELECTRICS, AND ALTERNATIVES, OH MY!

ENERGY SOURCES FOR THE FUTURE

Before the gasoline-fueled engine became the standard method of vehicle propulsion, early pioneers experimented with a large variety of alternatives. The huge success of the Ford Motor Company and its Model T, however, revolutionized the industry and cemented the future of the gasoline engine for the next century. Rather than continue to explore and develop alternatives, almost all manufacturers switched their focus to competing with the market leader in an attempt to gain market share.

As oil reserves became more abundant, and drilling techniques improved to allow for exploration in more territory, the 20th century saw the oil industry soar and oil become the most valuable commodity on the planet. Many international conflicts arose as nations went to great lengths to protect their supplies, with seemingly scant regard for exploring alternatives to the finite resource.

Renewed interest in alternative energy has grown, however, in response to endless oil crises, environmental damage, the finite nature of oil, and other political, cultural, and ethical considerations.

Railways led the way by focusing on electric power, and electric light rail began to reappear in cityscapes, having largely disappeared decades earlier as it was replaced by gas-fueled buses. In the late 1980s many of the automakers once again began exploring electric power.

The California Air Resources Board passed the Zero-Emissions Vehicle (ZEV) legislation in 1990, requiring all of the major auto manufacturers to develop and retail an electric vehicle. Although General Motors, Ford, Chrysler, Honda, Nissan, and Toyota all complied with the mandate, and between them reportedly developed 5,000 electric cars, consumer demand simply never materialized.

Many Californians claim they were unaware of the legislation or that the vehicles were even available, and those who were aware saw the technology as

STEAM AGE?

Steam is once again being tested as a potential fuel source. Steam engines for personal autos were created in the very beginning of automobile development but were regarded as too small to carry the needed water or the fuel to heat it. The Stanley Steamer had been a popular engine but was largely crushed by Ford's innovations.

either too expensive or untested. Battery life was limited to 60 miles per charge in the earliest vehicles, although the average car use by Americans was only 30 miles per day.

Regardless, the initiative failed, and many of the vehicles made were destroyed. Some were maintained in museums, but most went to the crusher.

Conspiracies as to why the failure was so sweeping have abounded. The oil industry is accused of using its lobby group Western States Petroleum Association to kill efforts to build public charging stations. Mobil, the oil company, in particular was accused of creating advertising campaigns denigrating the electric options in favor of traditional vehicles. Chevron bought patents and a controlling interest in Ovonics, leader in advanced batteries for electric automobiles. The implication, critics charged, was that Chevron bought the electric company to stifle its development.

The carmakers themselves were seen as actively promoting the status quo to avoid electric development. General Motors was accused of a negative ad campaign against electric cars. General Motors also seemed to have halted its electric program to focus on the gas-guzzling Hummer. Honda and Toyota were also suspected of having sabotaged their electric programs, even though both companies were heavily involved in electric light-rail development.

> In 2011 an impressive 85 million alternative-fuel and advanced-technology vehicles had been sold or converted. That number still pales in comparison to the number of vehicles in use globally, which is thought to be more than 1 billion.

Whatever the reasons for the failure of this early initiative, the development of alternate energy vehicles has gathered pace in the new millennium. Alternative-fuel vehicles have become familiar sights on American roads, and many automakers are investing heavily in exploring new technologies. Hybrid vehicles are traditionally gas powered, but the use of electric batteries and generators has improved fuel efficiency and cut emissions, leading to enthusiastic consumer adoption.

Many liquid fuels are being tested as gasoline alternatives, including dimethyl ether, ammonia, ethanol, biodiesel, liquefied natural gas, and liquid nitrogen, among others, all with mixed results. Hydrogen was an early success in auto production in the 19th century but was never pursued. Now hydrogen is seen as a potential future development.

To encourage consumer demand for alternative-fuel vehicles, many cities have created traffic lanes and parking facilities specifically for drivers who have made the switch. Parking spots allocated closer to amenities and city centers—often free of charge (or at least at lower rates)—have appeared in many American cities. Access to commuter lanes, regardless of the number of passengers or the time of day, has also helped encourage drivers to turn away from gas-guzzlers and look for better options. Charging stations for public use have become regular features of urban living.

IN THE TIME OF TESLA

MUSK MAKES A MOVEMENT

Named after Nikola Tesla, the Serbian inventor credited with pioneering the alternating-current (AC) coil engine, Tesla Motors has emerged as one of the leading electric-vehicle companies in the world. Founded in 2003, the company saw profit within 10 years.

Tesla was cofounded by Elon Musk, a South-African-Canadian-American, who had previously cofounded online financial services firms PayPal and X.com. Investing $100 million of his fortune, Musk started SpaceX, a company developing space rocket technology. Successfully creating the Falcon series of rockets, SpaceX has worked closely with NASA on a range of projects and has billions of dollars in rocket contracts from the agency.

Supercharging: Tesla began creating a network of charging stations to assist motorists who purchased its high-priced products. The 480-volt, fast-charging Supercharger stations have spread across the world, with more than 400 in place, including about 200 in North America.

LOG ON

Tesla doesn't make cars the way other companies do, and they don't want to sell them the same way. GM, Ford, and other car manufactures follow a system that dates back to the Model T—they use franchised car dealers to sell their cars. Tesla wants to sell their cars directly to consumers. This has led to several lawsuits as many states prohibit such activity. Online ordering, however, is currently legal in all 50 states.

Musk's exploration into rocket motors fired his ambition to develop alternative engine technology for automobiles, and five years after Tesla's founding, he became the company's chief executive. His own designs are integral to the success of the Tesla Roadster, a design based loosely on one of Nikola Tesla's concepts from 1882. Launched in 2008, the vehicle has sold more than 2,500 units.

The Tesla Roadster is an expensive, high-end product aimed at affluent buyers. This model followed that of previous innovations such as cellular phones, laptops, and flat-screen televisions, all of which were adopted widely by wealthy consumers at first, branding the products' images as must-have accessories. Eventually, pricing dropped to satisfy consumer demand, resulting in more widespread adoption.

Tesla also builds electric powertrain engines for other carmakers. Daimler and Toyota both feature models with a Tesla engine. Using lithium-ion commodity cells, Tesla's batteries are unique. The distinctive technology has raised safety concerns, which Tesla's management dismisses.

The success of the Roadster and S model has seen enthusiastic responses from formerly recalcitrant automakers. General Motors's Robert Lutz publicly stated in 2007 that the Tesla had inspired General Motors to develop a hybrid plug-in sedan, the Chevrolet Volt, which has proved popular. The Model X and the Model 3 are both in development or production, although delays with the Model X have held it back from its intended 2013 launch.

The network of Supercharger stations created by Tesla uses DC power to deliver 135 kilowatts, the alternative power system developed by Nikola Tesla's rival Thomas Edison. The charging systems themselves are generally powered by solar energy, primarily using SolarCity, run by Musk's cousins and a company in which he is a leading investor.

Although some models have been recalled, and incidents of fire from crashes have raised concerns, the Tesla safety and reliability record is very strong. Internal disagreements among the company's founders, resulting in acrimonious lawsuits, don't seem to have dented its successful trajectory.

DID YOU KNOW

Tesla has maintained open sourcing for its patents, meaning that they are open to public scrutiny. This transparency allows improvements from any user. Oddly, despite the open-source mandate, Tesla removed its patents from public view within its corporate offices.

NIKOLA KNOWS BEST

EDISON'S PROTÉGÉ, TODAY'S ELECTRIC INSPIRATION

Nikola Tesla, a Serbian inventor and electrical engineer, was born during a lightning storm in July 1856. Thanks to the storm, the delivery nurse reportedly declared Nikola a child of darkness, though his mother proclaimed him a child of light.

Early in his career, Tesla worked for Thomas Edison, helping develop direct current electricity generators, but Tesla quit the project to pursue his own theories and interests, primarily the alternating-current, or AC, induction motor. Most historians claim that Tesla and Edison were rivals, although the two did support each other through their careers, with Edison offering Tesla laboratory facilities after a fire destroyed his own. Tesla is often described as having a brilliant mind and imagination, but being slower at implementing his many ideas. One of his earliest concepts was a handheld device that would receive broadcast stock quotes and telegrams. Radar, X-rays, radio astronomy, and even a particle-beam "death ray" were ideas that Tesla formulated.

While experimenting with more efficient electricity, Tesla installed a high-frequency oscillator in his Manhattan laboratory that shook the building violently, leading many to assume an

earthquake had hit the city. His patented AC induction motor and transformer were licensed by Westinghouse, and the success led him to develop ideas for wireless lighting and electricity distribution. The rotating magnetic field was another Tesla success.

After his death in 1943, Tesla's work and flamboyant character became largely neglected until 1960 when the International System of Units honored Tesla by naming a unit of magnetic flux density after him. The tesla (symbol T) led to a resurgence of interest in the great thinker's inventions. His name now adorns the American automaker that designs and sells fully electric vehicles and features an AC motor directly descended from Tesla's original 1882 design.

TAKE ME HOME TONIGHT

WHO'S BEHIND THE WHEEL?

The fully automated car—a vehicle that requires no driver intervention—has been a goal for decades, with research and experiments being conducted as early as the 1920s. By the 1950s, promising trials had taken place, with the first truly self-sufficient cars demonstrated at Carnegie Mellon University's Navlab, and the Mercedes-Benz Eureka PROMETHEUS Project tested at Bundeswehr University in Munich.

Many working prototypes for automated cars and accessories have been developed by Bosch, General Motors, Nissan, Peugeot, Renault, Toyota, Volvo, and, perhaps most prolifically, Google. After the 2013 demonstration of VisLab's BRAiVE vehicle, which moved autonomously on mixed traffic routes open to the public, several states—California, Florida, Michigan, and Nevada—have passed laws permitting their use.

There are many perceived advantages to autonomous vehicles, though there are also still many concerns to address. Perhaps the most notable expected return is the reduction in traffic accidents, as increased reliability and the decrease in human error is expected to improve safety. Higher speed limits

Google's two seater self driving car being tested in a Silicon Valley parking lot

could be attainable, increasing road capacity and reducing congestion, allowing for better traffic-flow management.

Autonomous driving would alleviate parking scarcity, as vehicles could discharge passengers and park some distance away before returning to collect passengers. This would reduce the need for parking spaces within city centers and elsewhere.

Members of the community who are blind or face other challenges that prevent them from driving might be less restricted. Even intoxicated passengers, some proponents say, could be carried more safely, and there would ideally be no age restrictions for occupants. This in turn could reduce dependency on insurance and traffic police.

GOING GLOBAL

European cities are making plans for autonomous vehicle use. The United Kingdom launched public trials for the Lutz Pathfinder in 2015. Germany, the Netherlands, and Spain have also allowed robotic-car testing in traffic.

There are still many pitfalls and obstacles to be addressed before the nirvana of autonomous driving can be achieved. Software reliability would be a main concern, and should damage occur, where does liability rest? Communications and computer systems are known to fail, and the consequences of even a 99 percent "infallible" system could be dire.

Governments may be encouraging the development of prototypes, but a new legal framework and wholesale changes to regulations need to be adopted. Security concerns could increase, particularly in the age of terrorist attacks. A bomb-loaded autonomous car could be sent to any location to cause havoc.

Updated road infrastructure would need to be planned far in advance, and constantly updated mapping would be vital to ensure all vehicles operate under very specific conditions.

The impact on public transportation, such as taxis, would be huge. The number of job losses could be significant. In addition, if humans were no longer trained as drivers, would a passenger have any understanding of how to take control of a vehicle in the event of an emergency?

Although Mercedes, Daimler, and Tesla are all said to be close to full testing, or

> **In 2013** Google developed a driverless taxi named Robo-Taxi. The next year, a patent was granted for advertising-funded public transportation. Google has confirmed that it is looking into driverless public transportation.

have already revealed their potentially autonomous vehicles, the Google self-driving car seems to have attracted the most attention. The Google Chauffeur software that drives the electric vehicle has been developed at Stanford University, and the vehicle, named Stanley, has already won prizes for its progress.

In Nevada, Google's technology has been added to a Toyota Prius model as part of the experimentation, and it has been allowed on roads for testing since 2012. In addition to the few states already permitting the cars, the city of Coeur d'Alene, Idaho, has passed legislation to allow road testing.

Google's vehicles have already undergone many upgrades and alterations, with the removal of both pedals and the steering wheel from its latest prototype, which is scheduled for testing on San Francisco Bay Area roads in 2015.

Two crashes involving Google driverless cars are known to have taken place, but in both cases Google stated that the vehicles were under human manual control at the time. Complaints that no testing has happened in heavy rain and snow are major concerns, and how to handle sudden, unexpected traffic issues—not previously mapped—have to be overcome. Google admits these are challenges ahead, and the company projects a 2020 resolution date, somewhat later than the initial declarations that the vehicle would be ready for purchase by 2017.

JAY
DRIVING

LENO'S REAL LOVE:
HIS COLLECTION OF CLASSIC CARS

Famous as a late-night talk show host and stand-up comedian, Jay Leno has an unrestrained passion for classic autos of all models. He currently owns about 130 cars and more than 90 motorcycles, all housed in a former aircraft hangar near Burbank airport.

Leno's passions encompass any vehicle or engine that he is intrigued by, or those that achieved an engineering milestone. His hangar contains one of the most valuable and eclectic collections anywhere. Leno's enthusiasm for vehicles started with his purchase of a 30-year-old nonfunctioning Ford truck for $350 in 1964, when he was just 14 years old. One of Leno's first jobs was at a Massachusetts Rolls-Royce and Bentley dealership, where he learned the skills to get his decrepit truck running.

Every vehicle inside the hangar is still drivable, with its ignition key ready to go, but not every one is an expensive luxury vehicle. His McLaren Formula 1 racer, however, sold for $8.5 million when it was last available. The collection also includes a 1957 Buick Roadmaster Convertible and more than one Chevy Corvair. In 2015, Leno auctioned off his 2008 Dodge Challenger SRT8, raising more than $500,000 for military service members.

Other notable inclusions are a 1906 Stanley Steamer Cup Racer, a 1955 Packard Caribbean, a 1967 Lamborghini Miura P400, and a handful of vintage Bentleys from the 1930s. Other vehicles include various Jaguars in addition to lesser-known Bristols and Lotuses.

His passion for cars has found him back on television as the host of *Jay Leno's Garage*, a show in which he talks shop and shares his love for all things automotive.

WHERE WE'RE GOING, WE DON'T NEED ROADS

FLYING CARS? COMING SOON TO AN AIRSPACE NEAR YOU . . .

I n the same way that Herbie, the Volkswagen Beetle Love Bug, pioneered self-driving cars in movies beginning in the 1960s, flying cars have been featured in entertainment perhaps for as long as film and television have existed. Visions of a future where driverless flying vehicles would take everyone door to door were common devices for storytellers.

Some designers and engineers were focused on seeing how far current technology and future inventions could take them toward dream vehicles, perhaps none more so than John DeLorean, an executive with General Motors who later formed his own company, the DeLorean Motor Company. A maverick who had designed such classic vehicles as the Pontiac GTO and Firebird muscle cars, DeLorean left General Motors in 1973, though it took him eight years to bring his much-anticipated DeLorean DMC-12 to market.

Constructed from a fiberglass frame with a brushed-steel body, the car's iconic gull-wing doors gave it instant recognition. Yet despite the excitement about its release in 1981, the car was met with underwhelming sales. Little of the $175 million it had cost was ever recouped. Although there was a waiting list of buyers, production couldn't increase, and the firm went bankrupt after only about 9,000 were produced.

Of course, the DMC-12 never claimed it could fly or drive autonomously, but the vehicle holds iconic status and public affection as the drivable time machine featured in the *Back to the Future* trilogy. For the making of the movies, six cars were used in production, along with one made entirely from fiberglass for the scenes in which it needed to fly. It is now thought that just three of the models survived, two owned by Universal Studios. A number of other DeLorean models were later retrofitted to resemble the movie version, but alas, none of them were able to leave the ground unaided.

Futuristic cars were not new to cinema when the DeLorean became synonymous with time travel. In the 1960s cartoon *The Jetsons*, the family had been ferried to and from its Skypad apartment in an aerocar, a miniature space vehicle that needs no road system as it soars above Orbit City. Though the aerocar looked more like a glass-domed flying saucer than a flying car, Hanna-Barbera Productions, makers of the animated series, predicted many innovations during its 1962 production that are now commonplace. Perhaps the personal flying saucer will be among us soon, alongside the flat-screen 3-D television, tablet computers, home tanning beds, video chatting, and computer viruses, all of which the Jetsons encountered but were then pure fantasy.

The flying car is closer to reality than might be thought. Slovakian firm AeroMobil, led by designer Štefan Klein, has been working since 1990 on a vehicle that converts from road automobile to aircraft. After many decades in development, the AeroMobil 2.5 first took to the air in a test in 2013. There is not yet a confirmed release date, but suggestions are that 2017 will see the first AeroMobil on the roads and in the skies.

Meanwhile, American firm Terrafugia began working on an electric-powered concept in 2006, and although its first electric plane, the Transition, is expected in 2015, the team's next project—the road-to-air car TF-X—isn't anticipated until at least 2021.

Life often imitates art, and what the Jetsons and Marty McFly achieved decades ago may one day be a normal everyday form of transportation, not unlike the Model T.

A PARTING
THOUGHT

"The way I see it, if you're gonna build a time
machine into a car, why not do it with some style?"

—DR. EMMETT BROWN, *BACK TO THE FUTURE*

BIBLIOGRAPHY

Bak, Richard. *Henry and Edsel: The Creation of the Ford Empire*. Hoboken, NJ: Wiley, 2003.

Barnard, John. *American Vanguard: The United Auto Workers during the Reuther Years, 1935–1970*. Detroit: Wayne State University Press, 2004.

Batchelor, Ray. *Henry Ford: Mass Production, Modernism, and Design*. Manchester, UK: Manchester University Press, 1994.

Berger, Michael. *The Automobile in American History and Culture: A Reference Guide*. Westport, CT: Greenwood Publishing Group, 2001.

Boesen, Victor. *The Mercedes-Benz Book*. New York: Doubleday, 1981.

Boyle, Kevin. *The Ruins of Detroit: Exploring the Urban Crisis in the Motor City*. Mount Pleasant, MI: Michigan Historical Review, 2001.

Coffey, Frank, and Joseph Layden. *America on Wheels: The First 100 Years: 1896–1996*. Los Angeles: General Pub. Group, 1996.

Curcio, Vincent. *Chrysler: The Life and Times of an Automotive Genius*. New York: Oxford University Press, 2001.

Estrada, Chris. "Poll: Auto racing more popular in America than NBA and NHL." Motor Sport Talk. Accessed May 18, 2015. http://motorsportstalk. nbcsports.com/2014/01/26/auto-racing-more-popular-in-america-than-nba-and-nhl/

Fain, W. Taylor. *American Ascendance and British Retreat in the Persian Gulf Region*. New York: Palgrave MacMillan, 2008.

Foner, Eric, and John A. Garraty, eds. *The Reader's Companion to American History*. New York: Houghton Mifflin Harcourt Publishing Co., 1991.

Ford, Bryan R. *Beyond the Model T: The Other Ventures of Henry Ford*. Detroit: Wayne State University Press, 1990.

Georgano, Nick. *Beaulieu Encyclopedia of the Automobile*. London: The Stationery Office, 2000.

Lesch, David. *The Middle East and the United States: A Historical and Political Reassessment*. Boulder, CO: Westview Press, 2003.

Levinson, William A. *Henry Ford's Lean Vision: Enduring Principles from the First Ford Motor Plant*. New York: Productivity Press, 2002.

Lewis, David L. *The Public Image of Henry Ford: An American Folk Hero and His Company*. Detroit: Wayne State University Press, 1987.

Meyer, Stephen. *The Five Dollar Day: Labor Management and Social Control in the Ford Motor Company, 1908–1921*. Albany, NY: SUNY Press, 1981.

Nolan, Mary. *Visions of Modernity: American Business and the Modernization of Germany*. New York: Oxford University Press, 1994.

Poremba, David L. *Detroit: A Motor City History*. Mount Pleasant, SC: Arcadia Publishing, 2003.

Setright, L. J. K. *Drive On!: A Social History of the Motor Car*. London: Granta Books, 2004.

———. *Some Unusual Engines*. London: Mechanical Engineering Publications, 1975.

Shook, Robert. *Turnaround: The New Ford Motor Company*. Upper Saddle River, NJ: Prentice Hall Trade, 1990.

Singer, Charles, and Richard Raper, eds. *A History of Technology*. Oxford, UK: Clarendon Press, 1978.

Vachon, Paul. *Forgotten Detroit*. Mount Pleasant, SC: Arcadia Publishing, 2009.

Woodford, Arthur. *This is Detroit 1701–2001*. Detroit: Wayne State University Press, 2001.

Yanik, Anthony. *Maxwell Motor and the Making of the Chrysler Corporation*. Detroit: Wayne State University Press, 2009.

Yenne, Bill. *The American Aircraft Factory in World War II*. Minneapolis: Zenith Press, 2006.

www.bbc.com

www.businessinsider.com

www.cnn.com

www.extremetech.com

www.fia.com

www.formula1.com

www.history.com

www.investors.com

www.nascar.com

www.newsweek.com

www.npr.com

www.nytimes.com

www.ranker.com

www.sfgate.com

www.teslamotors.com

www.theautochannel.com

www.theguardian.com

www.time.com

www.wallstreetjournal.com

www.warhistoryonline.com

www.wired.com

INDEX

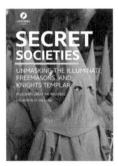

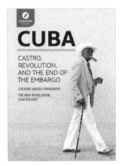